EUROPEAN
UNION
ALMANAC

EUROPEAN UNION ALMANAC

Handbook on the World's Largest Single Market Place

Godfrey Harris
with
Hans Jørgen Groll and Adelheid Hasenknopf

First US Edition

The Americas Group
9200 Sunset Blvd., Suite 404
Los Angeles, California 90069
USA

Swedish Trade Council
Translation and Interpreting
Services
Box 5513
S-11485 Stockholm
SWEDEN

Norwegian Trade Council
International Assignment
Services
N-0243 Oslo
NORWAY

ISBN:
0-935047-21-2

[ISBN for the 1995 Edition, *European Union Handbook and Business Titles*: 0935047-18-2
ISBN for companion book, *International Business Titles*,
in Sweden: 91-7548-362-9 and in Norway: 82-7217-065-5]

Library of Congress Cataloging-in-Publication Data

European Union almanac : handbook on the world's largest single
marketplace / [edited by] Godfrey Harris with Hans Jørgen Groll and
Adelheid Hasenknopf. -- 1st US ed.
    p.   cm.
    Rev. ed. of: European Union handbook and business titles. 1st US
ed. 1995.
    Includes bibliographical references and index.
    ISBN 0-935047-21-2
    1. European Union--Directories. 2. European Union--Handbooks,
manuals, etc. 3. Commercial correspondence--European Union
countries. 4. Job titles--European Union countries.   I. Harris,
Godfrey, 1937-   . II. Groll, Hans Jørgen, 1936-   .
III. Hasenknopf, Adelheid. IV. European Union handbook and business
titles.
JN27.E92 1996
341.24'2--dc20   96-6836
                                                         CIP

Printed in the United States of America

Book Designed By
Godfrey Harris [USA]

FOREWORD

This is the third edition of the *European Union Almanac*, expanding and updating information found in the first edition—published in 1994 as *International Business Titles*—and in the second edition, published in 1995, as *European Union Handbook and Business Titles.*

The second and third editions are a joint effort of the Norwegian Trade Council, the Swedish Trade Council, and The Americas Group and have been primarily designed to build greater understanding of the reality and importance of the European Union in the United States, Canada, and other non-member states.

These editions have also opened new understanding in international communications through a pioneering effort to translate business and professional titles in nine languages and by creating a first-time, English-language style guide for use in international communications by letter, telex, FAX, and on the Internet.

TABLE OF CONTENTS

TABLE OF ILLUSTRATIONS

HANDBOOK FOR THE EUROPEAN UNION

Background information,
current organization,
and salient data,
on the
European Union.

The Significance of the European Union

The European Union is now the single most important economic force in the world...

... Encompassing more than **370 million** people—

... Producing more than **$6.1 trillion** in goods and services—

... Involving **15 countries** operating under the same basic rules of commerce and governed by the same tariffs—an essentially borderless community to its own citizens and residents—

... Covering a territory of more than **1,400 miles** (2,240 km) from East to West and **2,200 miles** (3,520 km) from North to South—

... Working under its own **flag**, with its own maroon **passports**, its own anthem (Beethoven's *Ode to Joy*), its own international **monetary unit** (the Ecu, and soon the Euro), its own **court system**, its own universally and democratically elected **parliament**, and its own powerful **executive**—

... Conducting its own emerging **foreign policy**, its own large and comprehensive **foreign aid** programs, and its own embryonic **social initiatives**—

Although not a sovereign state in the traditional sense and still engaged in intense debate on many policy issues, the European Union nevertheless exceeds the impact of any other trading group in the world and promises to become an even more important factor in the fabric of global relationships in the 21st Century.

Because of this, everyone must now come to understand the functions and operations of the European Union as they have had to learn about Europe's individual states in the past.

The Members of the European Union

Background on the European Union

It comes as no surprise to visitors traveling through Europe these days that the French still speak French, the Italians still eat pasta, and the British still drive on the left side of the road. But these surface manifestations of the languages, cultures, and habits of Europe mask a profound number of economic and political changes that have occurred since the end of World War II.

Western Europe began organizing itself economically when six countries decided to coordinate the rebuilding of their war-ravished coal and steel industries. That brave beginning—involving Belgium, France, Germany, Italy, Luxembourg, and the Netherlands—required cooperation rather than confrontation. The resulting **European Coal and Steel Community** proved so promising that the participants soon expanded their cooperation with a second organization called the **European Economic Community**. Six nations had thus formed what came to be known as the Common Market to trade freely among themselves and to create a single list of tariffs applying to non-member outsiders. It was not long before some of those outsiders sought entry. The UK, Denmark, and Ireland joined in the early 1970s and Greece, Spain, and Portugal were added to the group in the 1980s. As the Common Market assumed a larger role in intra- and extra-European affairs, it took on a new name—the **European Community**. After some fifteen years, a new philosophical direction toward federation, another growth spurt, and yet another name change occurred. Austria, Finland, and Sweden joined an organization now called the **European Union** at the beginning of 1995.

What started out as a combination of two basic industries in six countries has now grown to a single commercial market with the same rules, regulations, and standards applying to all economic activity within 15 countries. Take environmental rules: Whether burning hazardous wastes in Italy or England, assembling electronic equipment in the Netherlands or Greece, building cars in Germany or Sweden, or tending vineyards in France or Spain, the requirements on how to protect the environment are the same.

In the span of just two generations, Europe has emerged from the devastation of an enormously destructive war into a single trading market that is larger than the United States and still growing.

European Organizational Development

Name Change Abbreviation—Year	Member State/Year of Joining
EUROPEAN UNION EU—1993	**SWEDEN** 1995 **FINLAND** 1995 **AUSTRIA** 1995
	SPAIN 1986 **PORTUGAL** 1986
EUROPEAN COMMUNITY EC—1973	**GREECE** 1981 **GREAT BRITAIN** 1973 **IRELAND** 1973 **DENMARK** 1973
EUROPEAN ECONOMIC COMMUNITY EEC—1958	**NETHERLANDS** 1952 **LUXEMBOURG** 1952 **ITALY** 1952
EUROPEAN COAL AND STEEL COMMUNITY ECSC—1952	**GERMANY** 1952 **FRANCE** 1952 **BELGIUM** 1952

European Union Organization

The Brussels-based **European Commission** is the European Union's most powerful institution. The Commission works under the direction of a body called the **Executive Commission**—the President and 19 Commissioners, all of whom must be acceptable to the member governments. The European Commission's staff—some 15,000 civil servants known as Eurocrats—are responsible for analyzing issues, recommending solutions, implementing policy, and monitoring compliance within the Union.

Commission recommendations for policy change are decided by the **Council of Ministers**—a body whose composition (and even its name) depends on the particular issue being discussed. When telecommunications are under discussion, for instance, the Cabinet Ministers from each country dealing with this subject gather in a Council of Ministers meeting labeled a *Technical* Council. On the other hand, when broad political issues confront the Union—a response to war, financial aid to a non-member—the matters are debated in the *General* Council. For contentious issues, voting is weighted with the larger countries having more voting power than the smaller ones. (See p. 19.)

The Council of Ministers is aided by a **Committee of Permanent Representatives**—ambassadors who maintain continuity for their home country's political leadership. Major political questions that cannot be resolved at the General or Technical Council level—the acceptance of new members, questions of a single currency, development of a common agriculture policy and others—flow to the **European Council**. This Council brings the heads of government of the member states together once every six months. A strict rule of unanimity applies in this body. Issues that might be vetoed by one or more states are discussed and compromise positions tested, but never put to a formal vote.

The **European Parliament** is independent of the European Commission and the two Councils. Its members are directly elected by the voters of each country from constituencies especially drawn for these periodic elections. Thus, a UK citizen today is represented by both a Member of Parliament in London and a Member of the European Parliament in Strasbourg. At the European Parliament, elected members tend to group themselves philosophically rather than by nationality. For example, the conservatives from a number of countries form one group, the socialists another. Although mainly a forum to gauge public opinion, the European Parliament has become stronger since assuming responsibility for overseeing and approving the Union's annual budget—now in the $100 billion range.

The **European Court of Justice** does not function as the ultimate arbiter of what statutes mean or settle questions of governance. Laws of the Union are enforced by individual member governments. Where there is a divergence in interpretation from one country to another or a case of non-enforcement of an EU law or regulation, the Commission brings action in the Court. The **Court of Auditors** is charged with monitoring how Union funds are spent by its agencies. The **European Investment Bank** grants loans and issues guarantees for capital projects to balance development among EU members.

European Union Organization Chart

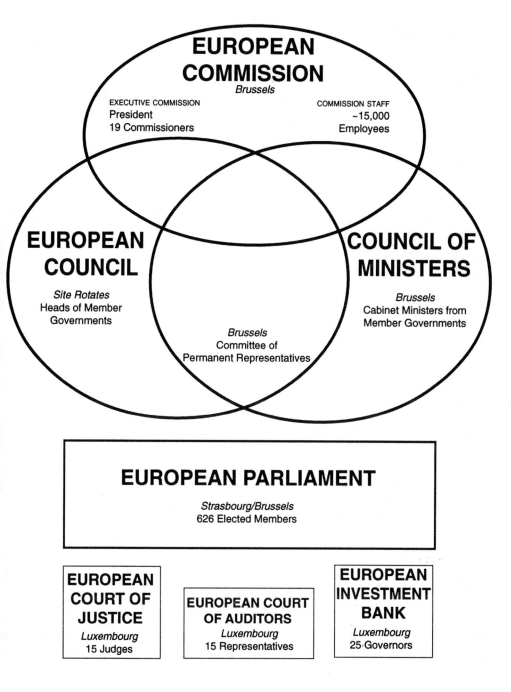

EUROPEAN COMMISSION
Brussels

EXECUTIVE COMMISSION
President
19 Commissioners

COMMISSION STAFF
~15,000
Employees

EUROPEAN COUNCIL

Site Rotates
Heads of Member
Governments

COUNCIL OF MINISTERS

Brussels
Cabinet Ministers from
Member Governments

Brussels
Committee of
Permanent Representatives

EUROPEAN PARLIAMENT

Strasbourg/Brussels
626 Elected Members

EUROPEAN COURT OF JUSTICE
Luxembourg
15 Judges

EUROPEAN COURT OF AUDITORS
Luxembourg
15 Representatives

EUROPEAN INVESTMENT BANK
Luxembourg
25 Governors

Executive Commission

All Commissioners serve 5-year terms ending in 2000.

President
Secretariat-General
Legal Service
Security Office
Forward Studies Office
Inspectorate General
Joint Interpreting and Conference Services

Jacques Santer
Luxembourg

Commissioner of External Relations—Vice President
Southern Mediterrean
Near and Middle East
Latin America
Asia—except Japan, China,
South Korea, Hong Kong, Macao,
and Taiwan
Development Aid

Manuel Marin
Spain

Commissioner of External Relations—Vice President
North America
Australia and New Zealand
Japan, China, South Korea
Hong Kong, Macao, and Taiwan
The World Trade Organization
Organization for Economic Development

Sir Leon Brittan
Great Britain

Commissioner of External Relations
Central and Eastern Europe
Non-member States of Western Europe
The countries of the former Soviet Union
Turkey, Cyprus, and Malta
Common Foreign and Security Policy (with the President)

Hans van den Broeck
The Netherlands

Commissioner of External Relations
Africa
Caribbean
Pacific
Lomé Convention

João de Deus Pinheiro
Portugal

Commissioner of Industrial Affairs
Information
Telecommunications Technologies

Martin Bangemann
Germany

Commissioner for Competition

Karal van Miert
Belgium

Commissioner for Employment and Social Affairs
Relations with the Economic and Social Committee
Equal Opportunities

Padraig Flynn
Ireland

Commissioner for Agriculture and Rural Development

Franz Fischler
Austria

Commissioner for European Parliamentary Affairs Relations with Member States (for transparency[1], communication, and information); Culture and Audiovisuals Office for Official Publications Institutional Affairs (with the President) 1996 Intergovernmental Conference (with the President)	**Marcelino Oreja** *Spain*
Commissioner for Science, Research, and Development Joint Research Center Human Resources Education Training Youth	**Edith Cresson** *France*
Commissioner for Environment Nuclear Safety	**Ritt Bjerregaard** *Denmark*
Commissioner for Regional Policies Cohesion Fund (with Mr. Kinnock, Mrs. Bjerregaard)[2]	**Monika Wulf-Mathies** *Germany*
Commissioner for Transport Trans-European Transport Networks	**Neil Kinnock** *Great Britain*
Commissioner for Internal Market Financial Services Customs and Indirect Taxation Direct Taxation	**Mario Monti** *Italy*
Commissioner for Consumer Policy Consumer Protection Humanitarian Office (ECHO) Fisheries	**Emma Bonino** *Italy*
Commissioner for Economic and Financial Affairs Monetary Matters (with President) Credit and Investments Statistical Office	**Yves-Thibault de Silguy** *France*
Commissioner for Energy and Euatom Supply Agency Small and Medium-sized Enterprises Tourism	**Christos Papoutsis** *Greece*
Commissioner for Immigration, Home and Justice Affairs Relations with the Ombudsman Financial Controls Anti-fraud Measures	**Anita Gradin** *Sweden*
Commissioner for the Budget Personnel and Administration Translation and Information	**Erkii Liikanen** *Finland*

[1] Transparency refers to easier access to EU official documents and data bases as well as greater availability of formerly classified material and better notification of work and legislative programs.

[2] The Fund provides financial contributions for the environment and trans-European transportation projects. Money from the Fund is restricted to projects in Greece, Spain, Ireland, and Portugal until 1999.

Directorates-General

Directorate-General I	External Relations (Economic/Trade Aspects)
Directorate-General IA	External Relations (Political Aspects)
Directorate-General II	Economic & Financial Affairs
Directorate-General III	Industrial Affairs
Directorate-General IV	Competition (Anti-trust)
Directorate-General V	Employment, Industrial Relations, and Social Affairs
Directorate-General VI	Agriculture
Directorate-General VII	Transport
Directorate-General VIII	Development
Directorate-General IX	Personnel and Administration
Directorate-General X	Audiovisual, Information, Communication, and Culture
Directorate-General XI	Environment, Nuclear Safety, and Civil Protection
Directorate-General XII	Science, Research, and Development—Joint Research Center
Directorate-General XIII	Telecommunications, Information Industries, and Innovation
Directorate-General XIV	Fisheries
Directorate-General XV	Internal Market, Financial Institutions, and Company Law
Directorate-General XVI	Regional Policy
Directorate-General XVII	Energy
Directorate-General XVIII	Credit and Investment
Directorate-General XIX	Budgets, Financial Control
Directorate-General XXI	Customs Union and Indirect Taxation
Directorate-General XXIII	Enterprise Policy, Distributive Trades, Tourism and Cooperatives
Directorate-General XXIV	Consumer Policy Services

Other Commission Offices

Secretariat General
Legal Service
Spokesman's Service
Joint Interpreting and Conference Services
Office for Official Publications of the EC (OOP)*
European Foundation for the Improvement
of Living and Working Conditions

Statistical Office (EUROSTAT)
Translation Service
Security Service
Task Force for Human Resources, Education,
Training, and Youth
European Centre for the Development of
of Vocational Training (Cedefop)

* Because this is a Maastricht Treaty Pillar 1 function, it retains its European Community name.

European Court of Auditors

The Court is an independent institution within the European Union. It ensures the legality and accuracy of all financial transactions and monitors how the Union's budget is spent and how its funds are managed.

Presidency of the
European Council and Council of Ministers
[1996 to 2000]

ITALY	January to June 1996
IRELAND	July to December 1996
NETHERLANDS	January to June 1997
LUXEMBOURG	July to December 1997
UNITED KINGDOM	January to June 1998
AUSTRIA	July to December 1998
GERMANY	January to June 1999
FINLAND	July to December 1999
FRANCE	January to June 2000

Weighted Voting in the
Council of Ministers

Austria	4	Ireland	3
Belgium	5	Italy	10
Denmark	3	Luxembourg	2
Finland	3	Netherlands	5
France	10	Portugal	5
Germany	10	Spain	8
Great Britain	10	Sweden	4
Greece	5	**TOTAL**	**87**

Issues of sufficient sensitivity to require more than a simple majority (8 of 15 countries in favor) must be approved by 62 votes (71% of the total of 87 weighted votes). If, however, as many as 23 of the 87 votes stand in opposition to passage of an issue, compromises must be sought within a reasonable period of time to achieve a Qualified Majority of at least 65 votes (or 75% in favor). In practise, however, controversial issues requiring a weighted majority in the Council of Ministers tend to be massaged over a 12 to 24-month period in an effort to find agreement on a compromise position.

The European Parliament

President   Klaus Hänsch

Group	Party Leader(s)	Members
European Socialists	Pauline Green	221
European People's Party	Wilfreid A. E. Martens	173
Union for Europe	Jean-Claude Pasty/Giancarlo Licabue	55
European Liberal Democratic	Gijs M. de Vries	52

Four other groups have formed with less than 5% of the members each. Members participate with these groups in Strasbourg and Brussels, while still retaining their traditional party affiliations in their home constituencies.

Parliamentary Seats

Austria	21	Ireland	15
Belgium	25	Italy	87
Denmark	16	Luxembourg	6
Finland	16	Netherlands	31
France	87	Portugal	25
Germany	99	Spain	64
Great Britain	87	Sweden	22
Greece	25	TOTAL	626

Source: Europe in Figures—1995

The European Court

President	Gil Rodríguez Iglesias	Spain
Justice/Pres. 1st Chamber & 5th	P. Jann	Austria
Justice/Pres. 2nd & 6th Chamber	F. A. Schockweiler	Luxembourg
Justice/Pres. 3rd & 5th Chamber	Claus Gulmann	Denmark
Justice/Pres. 4th Chamber & 6th	P. J. G. Kapteyn	Netherlands
Justice/1st & 5th Chamber	R. Joliet	Belgium
Justice/2nd & 6th Chamber	G. F. Mancini	Italy
Justice/3rd & 5th Chamber	Jean-Pierre Puissochet	France
Justice/2nd & 6th Chamber	Günther Hirsch	Germany
Justice/3rd & 5th Chamber	J. C. Moitinho de Almeida	Portugal
Justice/1st & 5th Chamber	D. A. O. Edward	Great Britain
Justice/4th & 6th Chamber	M. Kakouris	Greece
Justice/4th & 6th Chamber	J. L. Murray	Ireland
Justice/4th & 6th Chamber	H. Ragnemalm	Sweden
Justice/1st & 5th Chamber	L. Sevón	Finland
Premier Advocate	F. G. Jacobs	Great Britain
Advocate General	C. O. Lenz	Germany
Advocate General	A. M. La Pergola	Italy
Advocate General	G. Cosmas	Greece
Advocate General	P. Leger	France
Advocate General	M. Elmer	Denmark
Advocate General	N. Fennelly	Ireland
Advocate General	D. Ruiz-Jarabo Colomer	Spain

The Court itself decides which cases should go to a chamber of 3 to 5 judges and which are to be heard by the full Court. A Court of First Instance, created in 1989, generally hears all competition (anti-trust) and personnel cases. The Advocates General are charged with making "reasoned submissions"—legal and factual analyses based on treaties governing the EU— on all cases brought before the Court.

The Question of a European Currency

German Foreign Minister Klaus Kinkel has said that "European economic and monetary union is not just 'some idea or other,' but the central European political goal of the coming years." It will determine whether Europe continues toward greater political integration or reverts to being a trading entity. To gain acceptance and promote confidence, most believe that the new European currency—to be called a *Euro*—must be perceived to be at least as strong and as stable as the German mark.

To create the economic and monetary union (EMU) called for in the Maastricht Treaty, the economic performance of all member states will be evaluated in 1998. To qualify, inflation must be less than 3.7 per cent, interest rates may not exceed 8.3 per cent, government deficits as a percentage of gross domestic product must be under 3.0 per cent, and public debt must be less than 60 per cent of GDP. By 1999, the European Central Bank will be created out of the European Monetary Institute and the EMU will come into force among qualifying members. The new Euro currency will start circulating in 2002.

It will not be easy for Europeans to accept a new currency and have unquestioned faith in its lasting value. Among the numerous concerns being expressed are:

EMU 1996 PROJECTIONS

CRITERIA	INFLA. RATE 3.7	INT. RATE 8.3	DEFICIT %/GDP 3.0	DEBT %/GDP 60
Germany	2.0	6.4	2.8	59
Luxembourg	2.7	7.0	2.0	10
Denmark	2.5	7.4	2.0	78
Ireland	2.9	8.1	2.3	79
Netherlands	2.4	6.5	3.0	78
France	2.6	6.9	4.6	56
Austria	2.5	6.0	3.8	61
Finland	2.3	8.2	1.5	73
Belgium	2.3	7.0	4.1	136
U.K.	3.3	8.1	2.9	53
Sweden	3.5	9.3	6.4	86
Portugal	4.7	10.8	4.8	72
Spain	4.6	10.3	5.0	69
Italy	5.3	11.2	7.5	125
Greece	6.5	NA	10.0	128

Likely to qualify for EMU in 1996
Source: *UBS International Finance*, Autumn 1995

Legality Will the new currency be considered legal tender in all EU member states—whether or not the state is participating in the EMU?

Stability What ensures budgetary discipline within a country once it has qualified for the EMU? After all, the price of generating growth while restricting public debt has enormous political risks for leaders. The late Fall 1995 general strike in France was in protest to proposed restrictions on public expenditures for social programs—necessary to bring France into conformity with the EMU. The public reacted sharply and the government relented. What will happen when leaders have to tax, rather than borrow, to pay for social programs for a continually aging population? To solve the problem and build an enduring public confidence, Germany has suggested a set of new rules, including heavy national fines for excessive deficits, to ensure the stability and strength of the new currency.

Above all else, the EMU should be seen as a political rather than an economic matter. Resolving the political doubts, not answering the economic questions, will determine the EMU's fate and Europe's ultimate future.

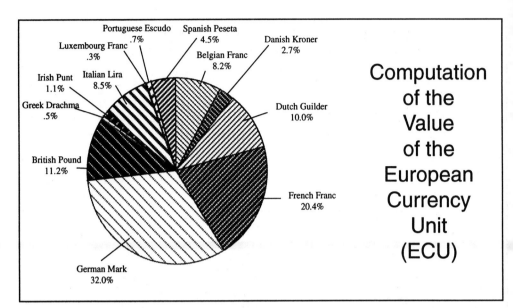

Computation of the Value of the European Currency Unit (ECU)

The Austrian, Finnish, and Swedish currencies are not yet included in the computation of the value of an ECU.

US$/ECU Exchange Rate

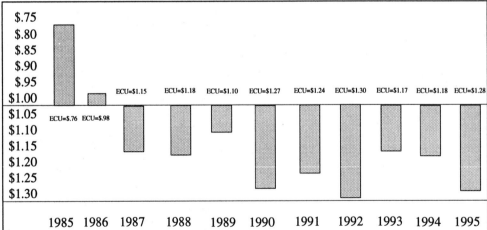

The value of the ECU (pronounced "*ek coo*," rhyming with "zoo") is listed in the Foreign Exchange tables of most major newspapers on a daily basis. While the ECU is mainly an international financial instrument, traveler's checks denominated in ECUs are available for purchase and are accepted throughout the Union.

European Union Income/Outlays

Approximate Anticipated Income/Outlays Between 1996 and 2000—
1995 Prices in millions of ECU

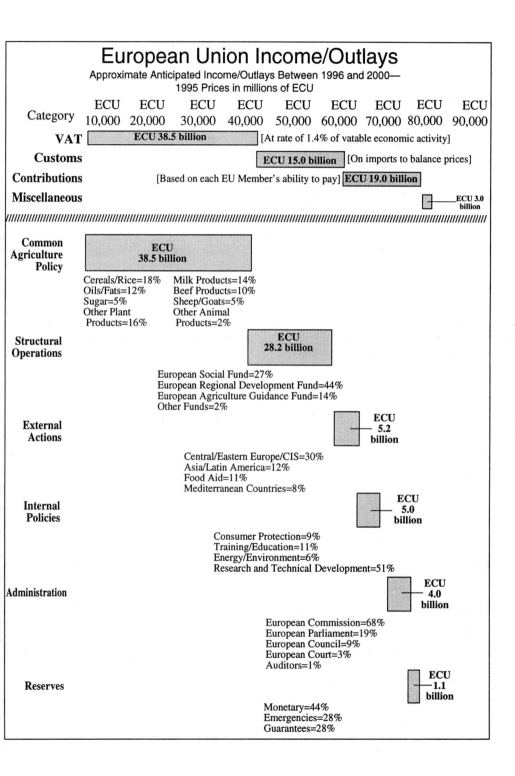

Category	ECU 10,000	ECU 20,000	ECU 30,000	ECU 40,000	ECU 50,000	ECU 60,000	ECU 70,000	ECU 80,000	ECU 90,000

VAT — ECU 38.5 billion [At rate of 1.4% of vatable economic activity]

Customs — ECU 15.0 billion [On imports to balance prices]

Contributions — [Based on each EU Member's ability to pay] ECU 19.0 billion

Miscellaneous — ECU 3.0 billion

Common Agriculture Policy — ECU 38.5 billion

Cereals/Rice=18%   Milk Products=14%
Oils/Fats=12%   Beef Products=10%
Sugar=5%   Sheep/Goats=5%
Other Plant   Other Animal
 Products=16%   Products=2%

Structural Operations — ECU 28.2 billion

European Social Fund=27%
European Regional Development Fund=44%
European Agriculture Guidance Fund=14%
Other Funds=2%

External Actions — ECU 5.2 billion

Central/Eastern Europe/CIS=30%
Asia/Latin America=12%
Food Aid=11%
Mediterranean Countries=8%

Internal Policies — ECU 5.0 billion

Consumer Protection=9%
Training/Education=11%
Energy/Environment=6%
Research and Technical Development=51%

Administration — ECU 4.0 billion

European Commission=68%
European Parliament=19%
European Council=9%
European Court=3%
Auditors=1%

Reserves — ECU 1.1 billion

Monetary=44%
Emergencies=28%
Guarantees=28%

Comparative Sources and Outlays of U.S. Government Funds

Fiscal Year 1996 Anticipated Receipts and Expenditures*
[in Percentages]

Average Anticipated Annual Flows Between 1995 and 1999
[in billions of U.S.$]

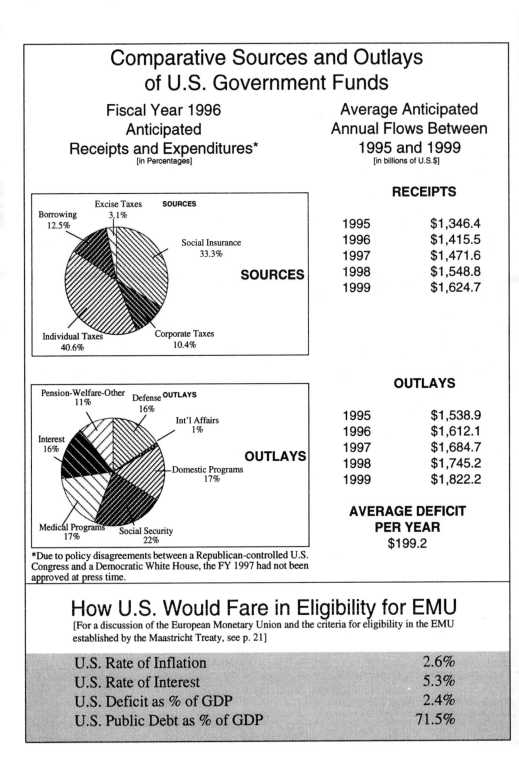

SOURCES

- Excise Taxes 3.1%
- Borrowing 12.5%
- Social Insurance 33.3%
- Individual Taxes 40.6%
- Corporate Taxes 10.4%

SOURCES

OUTLAYS

- Pension-Welfare-Other 11%
- Defense 16%
- Int'l Affairs 1%
- Interest 16%
- Domestic Programs 17%
- Medical Programs 17%
- Social Security 22%

OUTLAYS

RECEIPTS

1995	$1,346.4
1996	$1,415.5
1997	$1,471.6
1998	$1,548.8
1999	$1,624.7

OUTLAYS

1995	$1,538.9
1996	$1,612.1
1997	$1,684.7
1998	$1,745.2
1999	$1,822.2

AVERAGE DEFICIT PER YEAR
$199.2

*Due to policy disagreements between a Republican-controlled U.S. Congress and a Democratic White House, the FY 1997 had not been approved at press time.

How U.S. Would Fare in Eligibility for EMU

[For a discussion of the European Monetary Union and the criteria for eligibility in the EMU established by the Maastricht Treaty, see p. 21]

U.S. Rate of Inflation	2.6%
U.S. Rate of Interest	5.3%
U.S. Deficit as % of GDP	2.4%
U.S. Public Debt as % of GDP	71.5%

Preamble to the Maastricht Treaty on European Union

RESOLVED to mark a new stage in the process of European integration undertaken with the establishment of the European Communities,

RECALLING the historic importance of the ending of the division of the European continent and the need to create firm bases for the construction of the future Europe,

CONFIRMING their attachment to the principles of liberty, democracy and respect for human rights and fundamental freedoms and of the rule of law,

DESIRING to deepen the solidarity between their peoples while respecting their history, their culture and their traditions,

DESIRING to enhance further the democratic and efficient functioning of the institutions so as to enable them better to carry out, within a single institutional framework, the tasks entrusted to them,

RESOLVED to achieve the strengthening and the convergence of their economies and to establish an economic and monetary union including, in accordance with the provisions of this Treaty, a single and stable currency,

DETERMINED to promote economic and social progress for their peoples, within the context of the accomplishment of the internal market and of reinforced cohesion and environmental protection, and to implement policies ensuring that advances in economic integration are accompanied by parallel progress in other fields,

RESOLVED to establish a citizenship common to the nationals of their countries,

RESOLVED to implement a common foreign and security policy including the eventual framing of a common defence policy, which might in time lead to a common defence, thereby reinforcing the European identity and it independence in order to promote peace, security and progress in Europe and in the world,

REAFFIRMING their objective to facilitate the free movement of persons while ensuring the safety and security of their peoples, by including provisions on justice and home affairs in this Treaty,

RESOLVED to continue the process of creating an ever closer union among the peoples of Europe, in which decisions are taken as closely as possible to the citizen in accordance with the principle of subsidiarity,

IN VIEW of further steps to be taken in order to advance European integration,

HAVE DECIDED to establish a European Union and to this end have designated...their plenipotentiaries...

HIS MAJESTY THE KING OF THE BELGIANS
HER MAJESTY THE QUEEN OF DENMARK
THE PRESIDENT OF THE FEDERAL REPUBLIC OF GERMANY
THE PRESIDENT OF THE HELLENIC REPUBLIC
HIS MAJESTY THE KING OF SPAIN
THE PRESIDENT OF THE FRENCH REPUBLIC
THE PRESIDENT OF IRELAND
THE PRESIDENT OF THE ITALIAN REPUBLIC
HIS ROYAL HIGHNESS THE GRAND DUKE OF LUXEMBOURG
HER MAJESTY THE QUEEN OF THE NETHERLANDS
THE PRESIDENT OF THE PORTUGUESE REPUBLIC
HER MAJESTY THE QUEEN OF THE UNITED KINGDOM OF GREAT BRITAIN AND NORTHERN IRELAND

February 1992

The Maastricht Treaty involves three "pillars." Pillar 1 provides for economic and monetary union and supplemented the European Community's powers in the areas of the environment, research and technology, education, and training. Pillar 2 gives statutory authority for a common foreign and security policy. Pillar 3 deals with justice and domestic affairs including asylum, borders, immigration, and police cooperation. Pillars 2 and 3 are handled by intergovernmental cooperation among the Member States of the Union rather than by action of the European Council or the Council of Ministers. As a result, Pillars 2 and 3 do not issue joint publications.

All European Countries

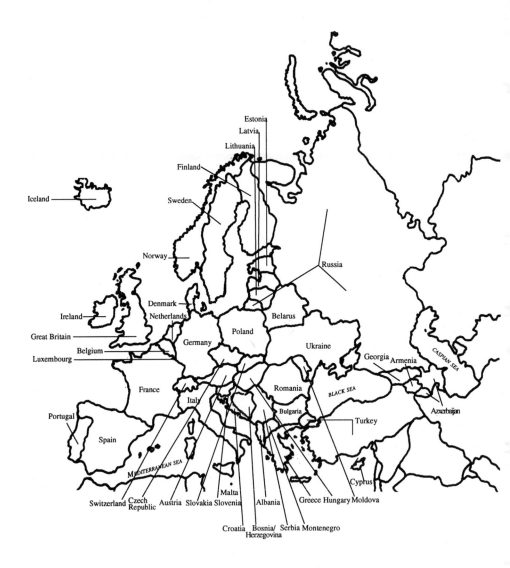

1995 in Review

☐ **Commission President's Agenda**
Jacques Santer of Luxembourg was confirmed as President of the European Union's Executive Commission in early 1995. In his first speech to the European Parliament he said that he intends to press three major efforts during his five-year term:
- Building a multi-billion dollar trans-European transportation network.
- Pursuing establishment of a single European currency.
- Forging a common foreign and security policy for member states.

☐ **European Union's Bosnian Experience**
A former European foreign minister once declared that members of the Union have created "an economic giant, a political dwarf, and a military worm." The European Union experience in Bosnia proves the point. Two EU mediators—High Commissioners Lord David Owen of Great Britain and Carl Bildt of Sweden—failed to find a formula for ending hostilities. Then, after a succession of military embarrassments for European forces serving under UN command, the United States convinced NATO to take a series of policy enforcement actions that eventually led to the Dayton Peace Conference's new borders and desengagement agreement.

☐ **European Union's Nuclear Experience**
In a second example of the EU's international disunity and how far it is from "forging a common foreign and security policy," ten of the 15 EU members voted against France's nuclear tests in a UN General Assembly resolution.

☐ **Fisheries**
While its *political* policies seemed in disarray during the year, the Union's *economic* efforts were strong. For example, it adamantly backed Spain's position in its dispute with Canada over how much Turbot could be caught in international waters. While both sides agreed to talk, no resolution had been reached by the beginning of 1996. In addition, the Union negotiated fishing catches with Morocco on behalf of the 15 members. To compensate Portuguese and Spanish boats for lost income, since the end of the previous agreement in April, the EU authorized a payment of $31 million.

☐ **Financial Support**
The European Union strengthened the European Investment Fund, a public/private program to guarantee loans and to provide venture capital to small and medium-sized businesses, by contributing ECU 90 million toward an ECU 200 million fund to guarantee loans to movie and television producers. The EU Financial Affairs Minister estimated the fund would provide a floor on ECU 1.0 billion in movie and television investments.

☐ **Agriculture**
The United States and Canada may receive compensation from the EU for lost wheat, rice, and other farm trade as a result of the Union's 1995 expansion. In return, the U.S. and Canada would drop a request to the World Trade Organization to

consider their complaint against the EU's new wheat and rice import tariff system.

☐ **Refugee Policy**
European Union policy toward refugees has been strongly denounced by the United Nations High Commissioner for Refugees and even criticized by the EU's own Commissioner for Immigration, Home, and Justice Affairs. At issue is the decision of the EU's Justice and Home Affairs Council to make individuals persecuted by *rebel* groups—even women raped in war as part of a conscious strategy—ineligible for refugee status in the Union on the grounds that persecution has to be perpetrated by an official organ of state.

☐ **Looking Back to the Referenda of 1994**
Norway is the only European country to have twice vote against EU membership— once in 1972 and again in 1994. As a result, interest in its independent course has been closely monitored. Interestingly, Norway has been obliged by the EEA Agreement to stay as close to major EU policies as possible—without being governed by them. For example, its economy already meets the criteria for the EMU. What it lacks is participation in shaping the policies it has aligned with.

Finland's Martti Ahtisaari said that one year after *his* country voted to join the EU, it "has lived up to our expectations." He noted that lower food prices, vitality in regional development, and Finland's stronger position within Europe have contributed to the positive reaction.

On the other hand, Austrian public opinion has now turned against the decision to join the Union. Austrians say that they did not realize the extent of the sacrifices that membership would cause people as their country works to conform to EU policies. Swedes have complained that a promised reduction in food prices as a result of joining the Union has not materialized.

How countries fare after joining the Union will be closely watched by political forces in the several European countries that have applied for membership and are trying to qualify.

☐ **World Trade Organization Implementation**
With the arrival of the World Trade Organization, the countries of the European Union had to change some of their procedures. For example, quotas had to be abolished in favor of customs duties. As a result, all citizens of the Union noticed a sharp increase in processed food prices.

European Union Flag

STATISTICAL CATEGORY	EUROPEAN UNION
POPULATION	372,161,000
Change	.37%
Natural increase	.10%
Net migration	.28%
Immigrants	10,400,000
Turks in EU	2,500,000
Former Yugoslavians in EU	1,140,000
Moroccans	1,090,000
ECONOMIC DATA	
Gross Domestic Product	Ecu 6,200,000,000,000
Importance of Trade	
Imports from the World	$759,623,800,000
Imports from USA	7.2%
Imports from Japan	4.3%
Exports to the World	$691,070,000,000
Exports to USA	6.5%
Exports to Japan	1.8%
Exports as % of GDP	8.0%
Balance of Trade/World	<$68,553,800,000>
Employment Factors	
Civilian Labor Force	146,459,400
Civilian Employment	131,946,900
Unemployment Rate	10.6%
Gov't Debt as % of GDP	70.9%
Inflation Rate	3.1%
Long Term Interest Rate	8.9%
SIZE	
Square Miles	2,021,875 [About 1/3 size of U.S.]
EDUCATION DATA	
Higher Level Secondary	26.2%
University Level	14.1%

ata adapted from 1995 documents from EuroStat

STATISTICAL CATEGORY	EUROPEAN UNION

EDUCATION DATA

Language Learning[1]
[1988 Data—Percentage of Pupils Studying Foreign Languages]

	FR	GB	DE	ES	IT	NL	PT	GR	DK[2]
	[A=100%-75%; B=74%-50%; C=49%-25%; D=24% to 5%; --=less than 1%; M=Mother Tongue]
Belgium (French)	M	C	D	--	--	B	--	--	--
Belgium (Dutch)	A	B	C	--	--	M	--	--	--
Denmark	C	A	B	--	--	--	--	--	M
France	M	A	D	D	--	--	--	--	--
Germany	C	A	M	--	--	--	--	--	--
Great Britain	A	M	D	--	--	--	--	--	--
Greece	C	B	--	--	--	--	--	M	--
Ireland	B	A	D	--	--	--	--	--	--
Italy	C	B	D	--	M	--	--	--	--
Luxembourg	A	B	A	--	--	--	--	--	--
Netherlands	C	A	B	--	--	M	--	--	--
Portugal	C	B	--	--	--	--	M	--	--
Spain	C	B	--	M	--	--	--	--	--

[1]Because the European Union's language data used here was collected in 1988, no information is available on Austria, Finland, or Sweden.

[2]See p. 51 for country abbreviations.

SOCIAL DATA

Television sets	477/1000 people
Private Automobiles	~95 million
Life Expectancy	
Males	73.6 years

Official Languages of the European Union

Danish	Finnish	Greek	Spanish
Dutch	French	Italian	Swedish
English	German	Portuguese	

NOTE: Austria speaks German; Belgium and Luxembourg speak French; and Ireland speaks English. The Official Journal of the proceedings of an EU body are kept in all official languages. For uniformity of references, the pages of each version are identical in subject matter.

Future Issues Facing the European Union

❑ **Maastricht Treaty Review**

The landmark treaty that established the timetable for creation of a single market and the establishment of a single currency also required an automatic review date for the treaty. The 1996 Intergovernmental Conference (IGC) will determine progress and review opposition toward creation of a more integrated federal European state. Britain and Spain have generally been opposed to ever increasing political integration, while France and Germany have generally been in favor of it. Here are the topics expected to be dealt with at the ICG:

- The timetable and further rules for establishing the EMU.
- Membership expansion—what countries will enter the EU and when.
- Common foreign and security policy, including majority voting.
- Strengthening of Interpol.
- Broader acceptance of the Schengen Agreement on border controls.
- Internal power sharing among the union's major organizations.

To insure that debate at the ICG does not split Europe, a "reflection group" has created the agenda and sought consensus on as many issues as possible. The Conference, beginning in Turin on March 29, 1996, is anticipated to continue for an extended period of time and take place in several different sites. Some fear, however, that it may become another "Euro-Go-Round"—endless meetings without results.

❑ **European Union Democracy**

The European Parliament's approval of the President of the Executive Commission and the 19 Commissioners chosen to serve with him, was seen by many as the first step in closing the Union's "democracy deficit"—the need to make the organization more directly accountable to the people of Europe. Many members of the European Parliament want to expand their institution's powers during the IGC, suggesting that they might use their veto power over the admission of new members as a pressure point in the forthcoming struggle for greater influence.

❑ **New Members**

The 5 members of the Central European Free Trade Association—the Czech Republic, Slovakia, Slovenia, Hungary, and Poland—are expected to be accepted for membership before the end of the decade. Other European countries—Bulgaria, Cyprus, Estonia, Latvia, Lithuania, Malta, and Romania, along with Croatia and Turkey, also hope to qualify for membership after the turn of the century. Non-member European states such as Iceland, Lichtenstein and Norway maintain a special relationship with the Union through the EEA, while Russia and Switzerland have separate bi-lateral arrangements.

❑ **Common Agriculture Policy**

The effort to create a common agricultural policy (CAP) for all member states—each of whom still subsidizes and supports its agriculture community in different ways—is a further impediment to further economic integration. The original goal of the CAP was to increase productivity to ensure farmers and ranchers a fair standard of living and to assure the availability of supplies for consumers at reasonable prices. Since 1992, the goals have shifted toward cutting agricultural surpluses, slowing the drift away from rural areas, and preserving the environment. The CAP accounts for about half of the Union's budget.

☐ The United States Position

The United States has maintained an important presence in European Union affairs through the North American Treaty Organization. In compelling an end to hostilities in Bosnia, it has reinforced its position as a key player in European affairs despite the reduction of U.S. troops in Europe from 336,000 in 1989 to 130,000 today. The U.S. action in Bosnia was even more impressive in the face of the resignation of Willy Claes as Secretary General and long before Spanish Foreign Minister Javier Solana was selected to replace him.

A list of NATO members not part of the European Union, EU members not part of the NATO structure, and EU members who participate in NATO follows:

NATO/Non-EU	EU/Non-NATO	EU/NATO	
Canada	Austria	Belgium	Luxembourg
Iceland	Finland	Denmark	Netherlands
Norway	Ireland	France	Portugal
Turkey	Sweden	Germany	Spain
United States		Greece	United Kingdom
		Italy	

☐ Public Opinion

A 1995 poll among 18,000 people in Europe found that two-thirds support the European Union with people in Belgium, Greece, Ireland, Italy, and Spain most positive and those in Great Britain and Sweden least favorable. In Switzerland, pro-European Union left wing parties found support in urban areas, while anti-EU right wing parties were favored by rural voters. In an Arthur Andersen survey of major companies in Europe, 70 per cent favor the EMU and a stronger Union.

☐ Travel

Border controls among the countries of Belgium, France, Germany, Greece, Italy, Luxembourg, Netherlands, Portugal, and Spain disappeared in 1995. Austria, Finland, and Sweden are expected to join the Schengen Agreement in 1996. Border controls for citizens from other countries remain in effect.

☐ EUROPOL

The structure and convention governing a European police agency—already referred to as EUROPOL—still eludes policy makers with the issue of how to handle cross border organized crime the most contentious.

☐ Looking South

To counter balance the emphasis of recent years on bringing more Central European countries into close association with the Union, Spain's term as President of the European Council culminated in a Barcelona conference involving the 15 EU members, 11 Mediterranean basin countries—Algeria, Cyprus, Egypt, Israel, Jordan, Lebanon, Malta, Morocco, Syria, Tunisia, and Turkey—and the Palestinian Authority. Libya was not invited to participate. At issue among the countries were questions of terrorism, political stability, illegal immigration, and freer trade. The EU has said it will provide ECU 5 billion in aid over five years for education and infrastructure development to the non-EU participants.

Directives and Regulations

Because of excessive and difficult to understand *directives* (European Union rules that have to be implemented through national legislatures and are subject to variations from country to country), companies within the EU have claimed to be at a competitive disadvantage from time to time. As a result, a determined effort will be made in the future to develop early and effective consultations to ensure that new rules are necessary and can be applied in a uniform fashion. A case in point is regulations dealing with smoking. For the record, a European Union *regulation* is a mandatory rule that must be enacted in exactly the same manner in each country and must be brought into force on precisely the same day.

Employment

By far the most intractable economic issue facing the EU is unemployment. A major initiative launched at the beginning of 1994 to create 15 million new jobs by the end of the century has made little headway. Economic growth is simply not producing enough jobs. With a 22 per cent unemployment rate among those under 25 years of age, Commission President Santer calls the situation "explosive."

Council Presidency

As Spain's presidency of the European Council was ending, Italy's Prime Minister, Lamberto Dini, began an intensive round of bilateral meetings with other EU members to discuss Italy's goals as Council President in the first six months of 1996. So important has this office become in influencing the direction of European policy that when Dini's technolocratic government fell, Italy's President sought a new leader to assume the office of Prime Minister to try to avoid Parliamentary elections before the EU summit convenes in Florence in June.

Commitment

Because most feel that without emotional commitment to the European ideal or a broad sense of community among Europeans, the nature of the Union's accomplishments seem fragile. Relatively few Europeans understand the workings of the Union, no more than 10 per cent of people aged 15 to 24 can identify the member states, and less than two per cent of EU citizens yet live outside their home countries. Ironically, the lone cultural thread that runs through Europe is *American*—including fast food restaurants, casual fashions, and pop music. Without heroes or any defining European moments, without responsibilities or consistent information, Europe may continue to be an elite ideal that receives popular support, but lacks much conviction.

STATISTICAL CATEGORY	AUT	BEL	DEN
POPULATION %<15 %>65	7,987,000 18% 15%	10,082,000 18% 16%	5,199,000 17% 15%
ETHNICITY	German (99%)	Fleming (55%) Walloon (33%)	Danish
LANGUAGE	German	Flemish (56%) French (32%)	Danish
RELIGIONS	Roman Catholic (85%) Protestant (6%)	Roman Catholic (75%)	Evangelical Lutheran (91%)
CITIES (% OF TOTAL POPULATION)	Vienna (19%)	Brussels (9%) Antwerp (5%) Ghent (2%)	Copenhagen (25%)
GOVERNMENT	Republic	Const. Monarchy	Const. Monarchy
GDP GROSS DOMESTIC PRODUCT	US$ 134.4 bln	US$ 177.5 bln	US$ 95.6 bln
GDP/CAPITA	US$ 17,000	US$ 17,700	US$ 18,500
IMPORTS **EXPORTS**	US$ 48.5 bln US$ 39.9.4 bln	US$ 120.0 bln US$ 118.0 bln	US$ 29.7 bln US$ 36.7 bln
% EU TRADE	~64%	~73%	~54%
BUDGET AS % OF GDP	45%	62%	58%
LABOR FORCE Agriculture Industry/Comm. Service	8.0% 35.0% 56.0%	2.0% 28.0% 64.0%	6.0% 20.0% 67.0%
LIFE EXPECTANCY Male BORN IN 1995 Female BORN IN 1995	74 80	74 81	73 79
OTHER NOTABLE FACTS	Hydroelectric power is important natural resource.	Belgian trade figures, by tradition, include data for Luxembourg.	Chief crop: Dairy products.

Data based on information taken from *World Almanac 1995*

FIN	FRA	GER	GBR	GRE
5,085,000	58,109,000	81,338,000	58,295,000	10,648,000
19%	20%	16%	19%	19%
14%	15%	15%	16%	14%
Finns (94%)	French	German (85%)	English (82%) Scottish (10%)	Greek (98%)
Finnish Swedish	French	German	English	Greek
Evangelical Lutheran (89%)	Rom. Cath. (90%)	Protestant (45%) Rom. Cath. (37%)	Church of England Rom. Cath.	Greek Orthodox
Helsinki (10%) Espoo (4%) Tampere (4%)	Paris (4%) Marseille (1%) Lyon (.7%)	Berlin (4%) Hamburg (2%) Munich (1%)	London (12%) Birmingham (2%) Glasgow (1%)	Athens (7%) Thessaloniki (4%)
Republic	Republic	Federal Republic	Const. Monarchy	Republic
US$ 81.1 bln	US$ 1.05 tln	US$ 1.331 tln	US$ 980.2 bln	US$ 93.2 bln
US$ 16,100	US$ 18,200	US$ 16,500	US$ 16,900	US$ 8,900
US$ 18.0 bln US$ 23.4 bln	US$ 250.0 bln US$ 271.0 bln	US$ 375.0 bln US$ 392.0 bln	US$ 222.0 bln US$ 190.0 bln	US$ 23.3 bln US$ 6.0 bln
~53%	~45%	~50%	~52%	~50%
50%	39%	43%	41%	40%
9.0% 46.0% 40.0%	7.0% 31.0% 62.0%	6.0% 41.0% 50.0%	1.0% 25.0% 63.0%	24.0% 28.0% 48.0%
73 80	74 82	73 80	74 80	75 81
40% of exports are forest products.	Europe's largest food producer, exporter.	Europe's largest country.	11% of trade is with USA.	Only 169 of 2000+ islands are inhabited.

STATISTICAL CATEGORY	IRL	ITL	LUX
POPULATION %<15 %>65	3,550,000 26% 11%	58, 262,000 16% 16%	405,000 18% 14%
ETHNICITY	Celtic	Italians	French German
LANGUAGE	English Gaelic	Italian	French German
RELIGIONS	Roman Catholic (93%) Anglican (3%)	Roman Catholic	Roman Catholic (97%)
CITIES (% OF TOTAL POPULATION)	Dublin (13%) Cork (4%)	Rome (5%) Milan (2%) Naples (2%)	Luxembourg (19%)
GOVERNMENT	Republic	Republic	Const. Monarchy
GDP GROSS DOMESTIC PRODUCT	US$ 46.3 bln	US$ 967.6 bln	US$ 8.7 bln
GDP/CAPITA	US$ 13,100	US$ 16,700	US$ 22,600
IMPORTS **EXPORTS**	US$ 24.5 bln US$ 28.3 bln	US$ 188.5 bln US$ 172.0 bln	(included in BEL) (included in BEL)
% EU TRADE	~66%	~ 58%	(included in BEL)
BUDGET AS % OF GDP	36%	40%	40%
LABOR FORCE **Agriculture** **Industry/Comm.** **Service**	14.0% 28.0% 57.0%	10.0% 32.0% 58.0%	3.0% 32.0% 65.0%
LIFE EXPECTANCY **Male** BORN IN 1994 **Female** BORN IN 1994	73 79	76 80	73 81
OTHER NOTABLE FACTS	Approximately 18% of imports are from the United States; 32% of exports go to GBR.	Chief crops are grapes and olives.	Tourism is 8.2% of total BEL/LUX figures.

NED	POR	ESP	SWE
15,453,000	10,562,000	39,404,000	8,822,000
18%	18%	17%	19%
13%	14%	15%	18%
Dutch (96%)	Portuguese	Spanish (73%) Catalan (16%))	Swedish (91%) Finns/Lapps
Dutch	Portuguese	Spanish Catalan	Swedish
Roman Catholic (34%) Protestant (25%)	Roman Catholic (97%)	Roman Catholic (99%)	Evangelical Lutheran (94%)
Amsterdam (5%) Rotterdam (4%) The Hague (3%)	Lisbon (19%) Oporto (14%)	Madrid (7%) Barcelona (4%) Valencia (2%)	Stockholm (8%) Gothenberg (5%) Malmö (3%)
Const. Monarchy	Republic	Const. Monarchy	Const. Monarchy
US$ 262.8 bln	US$ 91.5 bln	US$ 498.0 bln	US$ 153.7 bln
US$ 17,200	US$ 8,700	US$ 12,700	US$ 17,600
US$ 156.0 bln US$ 160.0 bln	US$ 28.0 bln US$ 17.5 bln	US$ 92.5 bln US$ 72.8 bln	US$ 42.3 bln US$ 49.7 bln
~59%	~72%	~66%	~55%
46%	36%	26%	48%
6.0% 28.0% 66.0%	20.0% 35.0% 45.0%	14.0% 24.0% 53.0%	3.0% 21.0% 38.0%
75 81	72 79	75 81	76 81
Almost 90% of population lives in an urban area.	World's leader in cork production.	Tourism accounts for 4% of the economy.	Forests cover approximately 50% of the country.

Glossary of EU Terms

Bridge	Biotechnology research for innovation, development and growth in Europe
CAP	Common agricultural policy
Comett	Action program of the Community in education and training for technology
EAEC	European Atomic Energy Community (Euratom)
Erasmus	European Commuinty action scheme for the mobility of university students
ERDF	European Regional Development Fund
ESF	European Social Fund
Esprit	European strategic program for research and development in information technology
Force	Continuing vocational training
Helios	Handicapped people in the European Community living independently in an open society
IMP	Integrated Mediterranean programs
Jet	Joint European Tours
Life	Financial instrument for the environment
Media	Measures to promote the development of the audiovisual industry
Phare	Poland-Hungary: Aid for restructuring of the economy
Race	Research and deveopment in advanced communication technologies for Europe
RTD	Research and technological development
Save	Specific actions for vigorous energy efficiency
Tacis	Technical assistance to the Commonwealth of Independent States
Thermie	European technologies for energy management
VAT	Value added tax

Euro Names

Not all names beginning or including the word Euro are necessarily connected to the European Union. For example, Eurostar is the name of a train that is a joint venture of the British, French, and Belgium railway systems; Eurocard is a private credit card operation headquartered in Sweden; Euro Info Centre is a Norwegian-government sponsored research facility providing information on the European Union to Norwegian and other businesses.

The EU Compared to Other Trading Blocs

The European Union, as an international organization, has been given sovereign responsibilities in many important economic areas that include law making and enforcement powers—powers that traditionally have only been claimed by national governments within defined borders.

The treaty-based and referendum-approved powers given the European Union supercede the individual powers of the member governments in those specific areas.

It is the supragovernmental nature of the European Union that separates it at the present time from all other international trading groups in the world. The other groups, enumerated on the following page, are basically intended to enlarge commercial markets through the gradual elimination of tariff barriers among member states. For example, the **European Economic Area**—now consisting of Iceland, Norway, and Lichtenstein—share the EU's commitment to the free movement of goods, persons, services, and capital; rules of competition; protection of intellectual property; and other commercial, social, and environmental matters. But the EEA represents only a free trade area. The European Union, on the other hand, is a customs union with a common trade policy and moving toward a common agriculture and fisheries policy and a unified monetary system.

World Trade Organization

The World Trade Organization—the successor organization to the General Agreement on Tariffs and Trade (GATT), founded in 1967—oversees global commerce by ensuring that all member nations adhere to the organization's rules of international commerce. If all signatory nations ratify the WTO treaty, the organization will consist of 124 member states.

European Union Investments

In the early 1980s, the members of the European Union invested four times more in non-member countries than in member countries. In 1989, a parity of internal and external investments had been reached: members invested ECU 34 billion in other members compared to ECU 33 billion in non-members. By 1992, the intra-European Union investments was twic the investments in non-member countries: ECU 38 billion to ECU 15 billion.

Principal Regional Trading and Economic Blocs

ANDEAN GROUP

Founded	1969
Goal	Economic integration.
Bolivia	Peru
Colombia	Venezuela
Ecuador	

APEC
Asia-Pacific Economic Cooperation

Founded	1989
Goal	Free trade among members by 2020.
Australia	Mexico
Canada	New Zealand
Chile	Papua New Guinea
China	Philippines
Hong Kong	Singapore
Indonesia	South Korea
Japan	Thailand
Malaysia	United States

ASEAN
Association of Southeast Asian Nations

Founded	1987
Goal	Economic and cultural cooperation with preferential duties on many products.
Brunei	Philippines
Indonesia	Singapore
Malaysia	Thailand

CARICOM
Caribbean Community and Common Market

Founded	1973
Goal	Promotion of economic integration among members.
Antigua	Jamaica
The Bahamas	Montserrat
Barbados	St. Kitts-Nevis
Belize	St. Lucia
Dominica	St. Vincent and the
Grenada	Grenadines
Guyana	Trinidad and Tobago

CENTRAL AMERICAN COMMON MARKET

Founded	1960
Goal	Elimination of tariffs.
Costa Rica	Honduras
El Salvador	Nicaragua
Guatemala	

CEFTA
Central European Free Trade Association

Founded	1996
Goal	Strengthen eligibility for EU.
Czech Republic	Slovakia
Hungary	Slovenia
Poland	

CER
Australia-New Zealand Economic Relations

Founded	1983
Goal	Free trade zone. Harmonized standards, customs procedures, and business laws.
Australia	New Zealand

EEA
European Economic Area

Founded	1994
Goal	Trade linkage to EU.
Iceland	Norway
Lichtenstein	

EFTA
European Free Trade Area

Founded	1960
Goal	Free trade among members.
Iceland	Switzerland
Norway	

G-7 SUMMITS
Group of Seven

Founded	1975
Goal	Discussions of longer range political and economic issues.
Canada	Japan
France	United States
Germany	United Kingdom
Italy	(Russia: Potential Member)

MERCOSUR
Southern Common Market

Founded	1991
Goal	Elimination of tariff barriers among member states.
Argentina	Paraguay
Brazil	Uruguay

NAFTA
North American Free Trade Agreement

Founded	1994
Goal	Elimination of tariff barriers by 2014.
Canada	United States
Mexico	(Chile: Invited to join)

SADC
Southern African Development Community

Founded	1979
Goal	Regional development.
Angola	South Africa
Botswana	Swaziland
Lesotho	Tanzania
Malawi	Zambia
Mozambique	Zimbabwe
Namibia	

Comparing US and NAFTA with the European Union

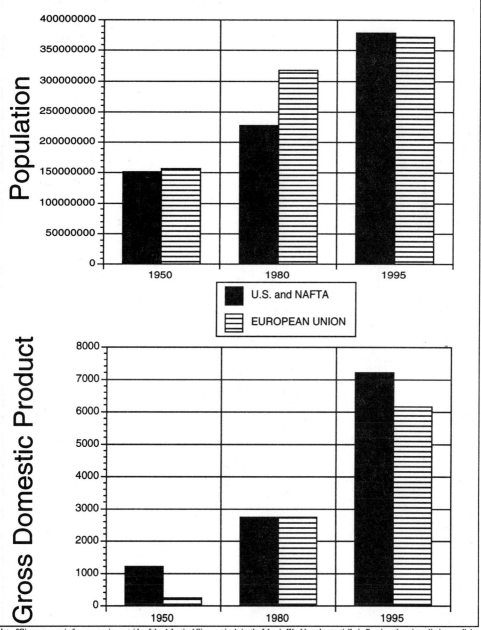

Note: °Given economic forces growing outside of the Atlantic Alliance—in Asia, the Islamic World, and potentially in Russia—there is preliminary talk in the United States about forming something called TAFTA—the Transatlantic Free Trade Area—to link the economic interests of NAFTA and the EU.

European Union Public Holidays

While there is some uniformity among the 15 member states of the Economic Union concerning public holidays, each country follows its own traditions.

In general, public holidays in Europe that fall on a Saturday are observed the preceding Friday; holidays occurring on a Sunday are usually observed the following Monday. Many offices close at mid-day on the day before a major three- or four-day holiday period or the day before or after a single day mid-week holiday.

Some religious holidays fall on the same day each year. Others, of course, move according to a formula governed by the traditions of each religion. Many countries have adopted religious holidays as national holidays—notably Christmas, Good Friday, and Easter in those countries with predominantly Christian populations.

Major Jewish holidays fall according to the Jewish calendar and generally occur in the Spring and Fall each year: Passover, in late March or early April, and Rosh Hashanah and Yom Kimpur, in September and October. The dates of major Islamic holidays— Ramadan, the New Year, and the Prophet's Birthday—are based on a lunar calendar calculation and occur at different times from year to year. As a result, and also because of regional holidays within each country, be sure to consult a current year calendar or contact the Embassy of an EU country (see p. 55 or 56) to determine the precise dates when contacts may be absent and/or particular institutions may be closed.

The holiday dates recorded on the following pages are based on a 1996 calendar. Some holidays will occur on different dates in subsequent years. Country abbreviations shown in *italics* signify a religious-based holiday, rather than a cultural or politically-oriented holiday.

January

Sunday	Monday	Tuesday	Wednesday	Thursday	Friday	Saturday
	AUT GRE POR BEL GBR ESP DEN IRL SWE FIN ITA FRA LUX GER NED 1	ESP GBR IRL 2	3	4	5	AUT ESP GRE SWE ITA 6
7	8	9	10	11	12	13
14	15	16	17	18	19	20
21	22	23	24	25	26	27
28	29	30	31			

February

Sunday	Monday	Tuesday	Wednesday	Thursday	Friday	Saturday
				1	2	3
4	5	6	7	8	9	10
11	12	13	14	15	16	17
18	19	POR 20	21	22	23	24
25	26	27	28	29		

oliday information derived from European date diaries.

March

Sunday	Monday	Tuesday	Wednesday	Thursday	Friday	Saturday
					1	2
3	GRE 4	5	6	7	8	9
10	11	12	13	14	15	16
IRL 17	*IRL* 18	19	20	21	22	GRE 23
24	25	26	27	28	29	30
Daylight Time Begins in EU: + 1 hour 31						

April

Sunday	Monday	Tuesday	Wednesday	Thursday	Friday	Saturday
	1	2	3	*DEN* *ESP* 4	*AUT GBR POR* *BEL GRE ESP* *DEN IRL SWE* *FIN ITA* *FRA LUX* *GER NED* 5	6
7	*AUT GBR POR* *BEL GRE ESP* *DEN IRL SWE* *FIN ITA* *FRA LUX* *GER NED* 8	9	10	11	GRE 12	GRE 13
14	15	16	17	18	19	20
21	22	23	24	ITA POR 25	26	27
28	29	NED 30				

44

May

Sunday	Monday	Tuesday	Wednesday	Thursday	Friday	Saturday
			AUT GRE ESP BEL IRL SWE DEN ITA FIN LUX FRA POR GER **1**	**2**	DEN **3**	**4**
NED **5**	GBR IRE **6**	**7**	FRA **8**	**9**	**10**	**11**
12	**13**	**14**	**15**	AUT GER BEL LUX DEN NED FIN ESP FRA SWE **16**	**17**	**18**
19	**20**	**21**	**22**	**23**	**24**	**25**
26	AUT NED DEN ESP FRA SWE GBR LUX **27**	**28**	**29**	**30**	**31**	

June

Sunday	Monday	Tuesday	Wednesday	Thursday	Friday	Saturday
						1
2	AUT IRL BEL LUX DEN NED FRA ESP GER SWE **3**	**4**	DEN GBR **5**	AUT POR ESP **6**	**7**	**8**
9	POR **10**	**11**	**12**	**13**	**14**	**15**
16	**17**	**18**	**19**	**20**	**21**	FIN SWE **22**
LUX **23**	**24**	**25**	BEL **26**	**27**	**28**	**29**
30						

July

Sunday	Monday	Tuesday	Wednesday	Thursday	Friday	Saturday
	1	2	3	4	5	6
7	8	9	10	11	12	13
FRA 14	15	16	NED 17	18	19	20
BEL 21	22	ESP 23	24	25	26	27
28	GRE 29	30	31			

August

Sunday	Monday	Tuesday	Wednesday	Thursday	Friday	Saturday
				1	2	3
4	IRL 5	6	7	8	9	10
11	12	13	14	AUT ITA BEL LUX FRA POR GRE ESP 15	16	17
18	19	20	21	22	23	24
25	GBR 26	27	28	29	30	31

September

Sunday	Monday	Tuesday	Wednesday	Thursday	Friday	Saturday
1	2	3	4	5	6	7
8	9	10	11	12	13	14
15	16	17	18	19	20	21
22	23	24	25	26	27	28
29	30					

October

Sunday	Monday	Tuesday	Wednesday	Thursday	Friday	Saturday
		GER 1	2	3	4	POR 5
6	7	8	9	10	11	ESP 12
13	14	15	16	17	18	19
20	21	22	23	24	25	AUS 26
Standard Time Begins in EU - 1 hour 27	GRE IRL 28	29	30	31		

November

Sunday	Monday	Tuesday	Wednesday	Thursday	Friday	Saturday
					AUT LUX BEL POR FRA ESP ITA **1**	BEL FIN SWE **2**
3	**4**	**5**	**6**	**7**	**8**	**9**
10	BEL FRA **11**	**12**	**13**	**14**	**15**	**16**
17	**18**	**19**	**20**	**21**	GER **22**	**23**
24	**25**	**26**	**27**	**28**	**29**	**30**

December

Sunday	Monday	Tuesday	Wednesday	Thursday	Friday	Saturday
POR **1**	**2**	**3**	**4**	**5**	FIN ESP **6**	**7**
AUT ESP ITA POR **8**	**9**	**10**	**11**	**12**	**13**	**14**
15	**16**	**17**	**18**	**19**	**20**	**21**
22	**23**	**24**	AUT GBR POR BEL GRE ESP DEN IRL SWE FIN ITA FRA LUX GER NED **25**	AUT GRE DEN IRL FIN ITA FRA LUX GER NED GBR SWE **26**	**27**	**28**
FIN SWE **29**	**30**	**31**				

European Union Telephone Codes

Country / City	City Code	Access Code
Austria	43	900
Vienna	222	[Vienna only] 00
Innsbruck	5222	
Belgium	32	00
Brussels	2	
Antwerp	3	
Denmark	45	00
Copenhagen	1 or 2	
Aalborg	8	
Finland	358	990
Helsinki	0	
Tampere	31	
France	33	19
Paris	1	
Marseille	91	
Lyon	7	
Strasbourg	88	
Germany	49	00
Berlin	30	
Hamburg	40	
Munich	89	
Bonn	228	
Great Britain	44	00
London	171 or 181	
Birmingham	21	
Glasgow	41	
Greece	30	00
Athens	1	
Thessaloniki	31	
Ireland	353	00
Dublin	1	
Cork	21	
Italy	39	00
Rome	6	
Milan	2	
Naples	81	
Luxembourg	352	00
Luxembourg	(No City Code)	
Netherlands	31	0
Amsterdam	20	
Rotterdam	10	
The Hague	70	
Portugal	351	0
Lisbon	1	
Oporto	2	
Spain	34	07
Madrid	1	
Barcelona	3	
Valencia	6	
Sweden	46	009
Stockholm	8	
Gothenburg	31	

Time Zones

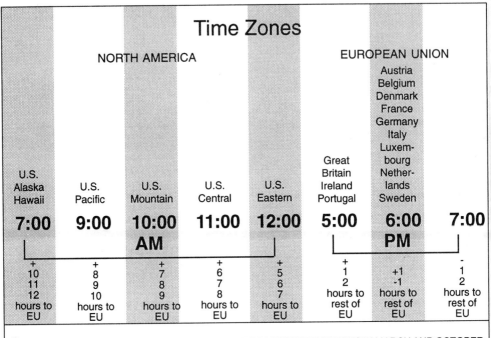

U.S. Alaska Hawaii	U.S. Pacific	U.S. Mountain	U.S. Central	U.S. Eastern	Great Britain Ireland Portugal	Austria Belgium Denmark France Germany Italy Luxem- bourg Nether- lands Sweden	
7:00	**9:00**	**10:00**	**11:00**	**12:00**	**5:00**	**6:00**	**7:00**
		AM				**PM**	
+ 10 11 12 hours to EU	+ 8 9 10 hours to EU	+ 7 8 9 hours to EU	+ 6 7 8 hours to EU	+ 5 6 7 hours to EU	+ 1 2 hours to rest of EU	+1 -1 hours to rest of EU	- 1 2 hours to rest of EU

[NOTE: BECAUSE SUMMER TIME BEGINS AND ENDS IN DIFFERENT WEEKS IN MARCH AND OCTOBER EACH YEAR, THE TIME DIFFERENTIAL BETWEEN EUROPEAN UNION COUNTRIES AND VARIOUS REGIONS OF THE UNITED STATES MAY AT TIMES BE AN HOUR LESS OR GREATER THAN SHOWN.]

Retail Closing Times

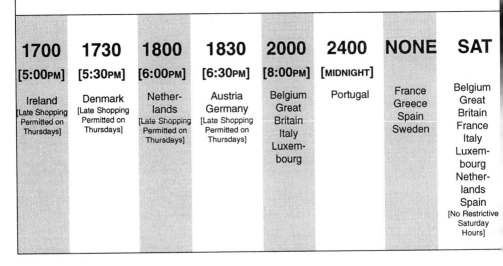

1700	1730	1800	1830	2000	2400	NONE	SAT
[5:00PM]	[5:30PM]	[6:00PM]	[6:30PM]	[8:00PM]	[MIDNIGHT]		
Ireland [Late Shopping Permitted on Thursdays]	Denmark [Late Shopping Permitted on Thursdays]	Nether- lands [Late Shopping Permitted on Thursdays]	Austria Germany [Late Shopping Permitted on Thursdays]	Belgium Great Britain Italy Luxem- bourg	Portugal	France Greece Spain Sweden	Belgium Great Britain France Italy Luxem- bourg Nether- lands Spain [No Restrictive Saturday Hours]

European Union
Identification Codes and Abbreviations

There are various codes to differentiate one European country from another. Here are four: **Currency codes** (used increasingly instead of symbols to identify currency types), **vehicle codes** (used on cars and trucks to identify the country of registration), **Olympic codes,** used by the International Olympic Committee and many other international organizations in their communications, and **VAT codes,** to differentiate tax receipts.

Country	Currency	Vehicles	Olympics	VAT
Austria	ATS [Shillings]*	A	AUT	AT
Belgium	BEF [Francs]*	B	BEL	BE
Denmark	DKK [Kroner]*	DK	DEN	DK
Finland	FIM [Marks]	SF	FIN	FI
France	FRF [Francs]*	F	FRA	FR
Germany	DEM [Marks]*	G	GER	DE
Great Britain	GBP [Pounds]	GB	GBR	GB
Greece	GRD [Drachmas]	GR	GRE	EL
Ireland	IEP [Punts]*	IRL	IRL	IR
Italy	ITL [Lira]	I	ITA	IT
Luxembourg	BEF [Francs]*	L	LUX	LU
Netherlands	NLG [Guilders]*	NL	NED	NL
Portugal	PTE [Escudos]*	P	POR	PT
Spain	ESP [Pesetas]*	E	ESP	ES
Sweden	SEK [Kronor]	S	SWE	SE

* Indicates that the country's currency is part of the European Exchange Rate Mechanism, a system designed to keep currency values within a 15% range above or below a rate fixed against the DEM.

How to Do Business Within the European Union

Because of the European Union's market size and because of its generous support mechanisms—and given its anticipated growth and expanded powers in the years to come—most outside commercial enterprises will have to come to grips with the question of how to develop their business interests within the Union's regulatory walls.

Here are some of the issues each business entity will have to resolve for itself:

Location   Where within the 15 countries is the locus of demand for the enterprise's goods and services? Is the same location suitable for an administrative headquarters as well as manufacturing and/or distribution facilities? How do taxation considerations affect the decision, since taxation (other than VAT) is still a matter for each nation to decide?

Quality   Do the products and services of the enterprise meet current and anticipated safety, environmental, and packaging rules of the Union?

Information   Is the firm's current research capabilities and its corps of advisors sufficiently knowledgeable about Union affairs to provide timely information and recommendations on the political, economic, social, and legal environment to be faced?

Administration   Do the current personnel, financial, accounting, legal and other policies of the enterprise meet the requirements of the European Union and its member states?

These issues will be resolved more easily if decision makers accept the fact that over the past 45 years the Union has developed its own methods and its own bureaucratic culture, different in many respects from any of its member states and different again from what a business might be accustomed to.

Directory of Official Organizations

European Commission
Rue de la Loi 200
B-1049 Brussels
BELGIUM
☎ + (32) 2 299 1111
fx + (32) 2 295 0139

European Council
Rue de la Loi 170
B-1408 Brussels
BELGIUM
☎ + (32) 2 234 6111
fx + (32) 2 295 7381

European Parliament
Palais de l'Europe (Plenary Sessions)
Place Lenôtre
76006 Strasbourg
FRANCE
☎ + (32) 2 299 1111
fx + (32) 2 295 0139

European Parliament
Secretariat General
Plateau de Kirchberg
2929 Luxembourg
LUXEMBOURG
☎ + (352) 43 001
fx + (352) 43 70 09

European Court of Justice
Palais de la Cour de Justice
L-2925 Luxembourg
LUXEMBOURG
☎ + (352) 43 00 1
fx + (352) 437 009

European Court of Auditors
12 rue Alcide de Basperi
L-1615 Luxembourg
LUXEMBOURG
☎ + (352) 43 03 1
fx + (352) 43 94 2

European Press and Information Office
305 East 47th Street
New York, NY 10017
USA
☎ + (1) 212 371 3804
fx + (1) 212 688 1013

European Union
2100 M Street, NW- Suite 707
Washington, DC 20037
USA
☎ + (1) 202 862 9500
fx + (1) 202 429 1766

European Investment Bank
100 Bd. Konrad Adenauer
L-2950 Luxembourg
LUXEMBOURG
☎ + (352) 43 79 31 42
fx + (352) 43 77 04

EUROSTAT (Statistical Office of the EU)
Batiment Jean Monnet
L-2920 Luxembourg
LUXEMBOURG
☎ + (352) 43 013 4567
fx + (352) 43 64 04

European Ombudsman (Jacob Söderman)
Palais de l'Europe
F-87000 Strasbourg
FRANCE
☎ + (33) 88 17 23 13
fx + (33) 88 17 90 62

The actual physical location of individuals affiliated with the above offices may be different from the mailing addresses given above.

Directory of Sources of Support

CONSULTANTS

Arthur D. Little
Bd. de la Woluwe 2
B-1150 Brussels
BELGIUM
☎ + (32) 2 762 0285
🖷 + (32) 2 762 0758
Broadbased worldwide consulting firm with 350 consultants in Europe involved with EU-related matters.

Bates & Wacker
Rue du Moniteur 9
B-1000 Brussels
BELGIUM
☎ + (32) 2 219 0305
🖷 + (32) 2 219 3215
Legal and management consultancy, information dissemination, monitoring, and training.

Charles Barker PLC
Rue Montoyer, bte 2
B-1040 Brussels
BELGIUM
☎ + (32) 2 511 0645
🖷 + (32) 2 512 5344
Advice, research, and reporting on EU developments in law, food, finance, environment, tax, trade, transportation and tourism.

KPMG Belgium
Rue Neerveld 101-103, Bte 3
B-1200 Brussels
BELGIUM
☎ + (32) 2 773 3611
🖷 + (32) 2 772 3305
Worldwide business advisory firm specializing in strategies to minimize risk and maximize opportunities based on EU developments.

Van Luyken—
PR and PA Consultants
Rue Guimard 19
B-1040 Brussels
BELGIUM
☎ + (32) 2 514 3300
🖷 + (32) 2 514 3058
Specializes in EU financial resource programs, cultural, and agricultural matters.

WS Atkins International
Rue de l'Industry 4, bte 5
B-1040 Brussels
BELGIUM
☎ + (32) 2 502 0270
🖷 + (32) 2 512 1225
Fully integrated, firm involved in planning, engineering, and management services in most fields of concern to the EU.

LOBBYISTS

AEF-Harrison International
Av. Livingstone 33
B-1040 Brussels
BELGIUM
☎ + (32) 2 230 0645
🖷 + (32) 2 512 5344
Advice, research, and reporting on EU developments in law, food, finance, environment, tax, trade, transportation and tourism.

The Rowland Company
Rue du Commerce 20-22
B-1040 Brussels
BELGIUM
☎ + (32) 2 512 0919
🖷 + (32) 2 512 4120
Specializing in public affairs and public relations and operates from 17 offices outside of Brussels.

Trimedia Europe
Avenue de Tervueren 439
B-1150 Brussels
BELGIUM
☎ + (32) 2 762 4057
🖷 + (32) 2 762 2186
Lobbying and monitoring EU concerns from most important European cities.

INFORMATION

Editions Delta
Rue Scarlqun 55
B-1030 Brussels
BELGIUM
☎ + (32) 2 217 5555
🖷 + (32) 2 217 9393
Directories include Yearbook, Euro Who's Who, and Trade and Professional Associations.

Europe Daily
Bid Saint-Lazare 10, Bte 13
B-1140 Brussels
BELGIUM
☎ + (32) 2 219 0256
🖷 + (32) 2 217 6697
Annual reference directory on European Union facts.

Europe Information Service
Rue de Genève 6
B-1210 Brussels
BELGIUM
☎ + (32) 2 242 6020
🖷 + (32) 2 242 9549
Extensive daily coverage of news emanating from the European Union.

Euro Info Centre
Drammensveien 40
N-0243 Oslo
NORWAY
☎ + (47) 2 292 6570
🖷 + (47) 2 243 1640
Provides information concerning the European Union and undertakes more extensive research on a fee basis.

EuroConfidential SA
Rue de Rixensart 18-BP 54
B-1332 Genval
BELGIUM
☎ + (32) 2 652 0284
🖷 + (32) 2 653 0180
Its Directory of EC Information Sources identifies 7000 entities. Also publishes, Access to European Union, a comprehensive annual reference on the EU.

Unipub
4611-F Assembly Drive
Lanham, MD 20706-4391
USA
☎ + (1) 800 274 4888
🖷 + (1) 301 459 0056
Sales office for official European Union publications in the U.S.

The entities listed above are presented as a sampling of the firms and government agencies providing a variety of support services connected with the European Union. For law firms, see *Martindale-Hubbell® International Law Directory*, Vol. I.

Directory of EU Member Embassies in Brussels

AUSTRIA
avenue de Cortenberg 118
B-1040 Brussels
BELGIUM
☎ + (32) 2 741 2111
fx + (32) 2 736 8347

IRELAND
avenue Galilée 5, Boîte 22
B-1030 Brussel
BELGIUM
☎ + (32) 2 218 0605
fx + (32) 2 219 3449

BELGIUM
rue Beilliard 62
B-1040 Brussels,
BELGIUM
☎ + (32) 2 233 2111
fx + (32) 2 231 1075

ITALY
rue du Marteau 9
B-1040 Brussels
BELGIUM
☎ + (32) 2 220 0410
fx + (32) 2 511 5108

DENMARK
rue d'Arion 73
B-1040 Brussels
BELGIUM
☎ + (32) 2 233 0811
fx + (32) 2 230 9284

LUXEMBOURG
rue du Noyer 211
B-1040 Brussels
BELGIUM
☎ + (32) 2 735 2060
fx + (32) 2 736 1429

FINLAND
rue de Trève 100
B-1040 Brussels
BELGIUM
☎ + (32) 2 287 8411
fx + (32) 2 287 8400

NETHERLANDS:
Avenue Herrmann Debroux 48
B-1200 Brussels
BELGIUM
☎ + (32) 2 679 1511
fx + (32) 2 679 1795

FRANCE
place du Louvain 14
B-1000 Brussels
BELGIUM
☎ + (32) 2 229 6211
fx + (32) 2 229 8282

PORTUGAL
rue Marie-Thérèse 11-13
B-1040 Brussels
BELGIUM
☎ + (32) 2 227 4400
fx + (32) 2 210 1542

GERMANY
rue Jacque de Laiaing 19-21
B-1040 Brussels
BELGIUM
☎ + (32) 2 238 1811
fx + (32) 2 238 1978

SPAIN
boulevard du Régent 52-54
B-1000 Brussels
BELGIUM
☎ + (32) 2 509 8611
fx + (32) 2 511 5108

GREAT BRITAIN
rond-point Schuman 6
B-1040 Brussels
BELGIUM
☎ + (32) 2 287 8211
fx + (32) 2 287 8398

SWEDEN
square de Meeûs 30
B-1040 Brussels
BELGIUM
☎ + (32) 2 289 5611
fx + (32) 2 289 5600

GREECE
avenue de Cortenberg 71
B-1040 Brussels
BELGIUM
☎ + (32) 2 739 5611
fx + (32) 2 735 5979

UNITED STATES (Mission to the European Union)
40, boulevard du Régent
B-1000 Brussels
BELGIUM
☎ + (32) 2 508 2222
fx + (32) 2 514 4334

Directory of EU Member Embassies in the United States

AUSTRIA
3524 International Court NW,
Washington, DC 20008
☎ (202) 895-6700
℻ (202) 895-6750

BELGIUM
3330 Garfield Street, NW
Washington, DC 20008
☎ (202) 333-6900
℻ (202) 333-3079

DENMARK
3200 Whitehaven Street, NW
Washington, DC 20008
☎ (202) 234-4300
℻ (202) 328-1470

FINLAND
3301 Massachusetts Av. NW
Washington, DC 20008
☎ (202) 298-5800
℻ (202) 298-6030

FRANCE
4101 Reservoir Road NW
Washington, DC 20007
☎ (202) 944-6000
℻ (202) 944-6336

GERMANY
4645 Reservoir Road NW
Washington, DC 20007
☎ (202) 298-4000
℻ (202) 298-4249

GREAT BRITAIN
3100 Massachusetts Av. NW
Washington, DC 20008
☎ (202) 462-1340
℻ (202) 899-4255

GREECE
2221 Massachusetts Av. NW
Washington, DC 20008
☎ (202) 667-3168
℻ (202) 939-5824

IRELAND
2234 Massachusetts Av. NW
Washington, DC 20008
☎ (202) 462-3939
℻ (202) 232-5993

ITALY
1601 Fuller Street NW
Washington, DC 20009
☎ (202) 328-5500
℻ (202) 328-0636

LUXEMBOURG
2200 Massachusetts Av. NW
Washington, DC 20008
☎ (202) 265-4171
℻ (202) 328-8270

NETHERLANDS:
4200 Wisconsin Avenue NW
Washington, DC 20008
☎ (202) 244-5300
℻ (202) 362-3430

PORTUGAL
2125 Kalorama Road NW
Washington, DC 20008
☎ (202) 328-8610
℻ (202) 462-3726

SPAIN
2375 Pennsylvania Av. NW
Washington, DC 20037
☎ (202) 452-0100
℻ (202) 833-5670

SWEDEN
1501 M Street, NW
Washington, DC 20005
☎ (202) 467-2600
℻ (202) 467-269

UNITED STATES
Office of the European Union
State Department Building
Washington, DC 20520
☎ (202) 647-3246
℻ (202) 647-9959

INTERNATIONAL STYLE GUIDE

Styles in international
commercial dealings are
changing rapidly as economic integration
and high technology provide new ways
for business to get its work done.

The guidelines that follow are based
on the principle that
writers should try to use
syntax, grammar, and references
as likely to be familiar to the
recipient as the sender.

Adherence to this principle will help
facilitate greater understanding—
and increase efficiency through
clearer written communications—
with individuals in the European Union
and throughout the world.

Written Communications Checklist

☐ **Avoid the Use of Colloquialisms**
Unless you are sure that there can be no misunderstanding, avoid slang terms (*the whole nine yards*), sports analogies (*a slam dunk*), or current cultural references (*it'll be another Tail Hook*) when writing to foreigners.

☐ **Keep It Short, Sam**
When writing to contacts abroad, adopt another form of the old KISS selling adage— *Keep It Short, Sam.* Avoid compound sentence structures and exotic grammatical constructions wherever possible; try to use bulleted paragraphs and numbered lists; use redundant references when necessary to ensure clarity and precision.

☐ **Leave out the Superlatives**
While the use of superlatives—best, biggest, largest, oldest, most— are a common American way to describe a product, place, or service, they need a context to have impact. Foreigners may lack the comparative knowledge and miss the meaning being conveyed. Use statistics and other factual data to make the same point.

☐ **Double Check Everything**
When writing to someone abroad, be sure to review all English spellings, punctuation, references, agreements, and verb tenses to ensure that unintended errors do not send non-native English speakers to dictionaries and grammar books looking for something that may not even be there.

☐ **Use British English When Comfortable**
Because American English differs in many ways from British English—and most of the world's 750 million English speakers are taught British spellings and usage for written communication—try to adopt British "practise." For example, use *waistcoat* instead of vest, *petrol* instead of gas, *cheque* instead of check, *colour* instead of color.

☐ **Go Native**
Use spellings, names, and references as they are employed in the originator's country. Thus, a mention of the British "Labour Party,"

contrary to American newspaper practice, should not become the "Labor Party." By the same token, Hr Schmidt should become Mr. Schmidt.

☐ **Go Metric**
Use metric measurements when describing distances, temperatures, weights, and volumes. (See pp. 62-63.) When precision is not important, round off metric amounts to a nearest whole number—a 4 lb. package should be described as around 2 kilos instead of 1.82 kilos. When precision is crucial, give both the metric and U.S. equivalents.

☐ **Use a 24-Hour Clock**
Most Europeans and other foreigners refer to time on the 24-hour clock. To avoid confusion between AM and PM designations used with the 12-hour clock, always describe arrival and departure times in military terms. The easiest way to become comfortable with the 24-hour clock is to add or subtract the number 12 from all times after noon.

☐ **Define the $ Sign**
Because many countries call their local currency "dollars" and use the same symbol as Americans to differentiate monetary amounts from other numbers, always distinguish American dollars as *US$* in international communications. By the same token, if referring to Canadian dollars or Australian dollars use C$ and A$. While some continue to use traditional abbreviations to identify currencies—DM for German Marks and FF for French Francs—there is now a trend to using the three letter code of the international currency markets. (See page 51.) Unless dealing in a commodity always quoted in US dollars (gold, for example) or involved in third country dealings, try to refer to monetary amounts in the local currency of the recipient of the communication.

☐ **Nothing Under 10 Points and Wide Margins All Around on FAXes**
Transmit documents with a type face of at least 10 points in size. Because numbers often blur at the top, bottom, and edges of FAXes—leaving 5's looking like 6's and 3's and 8's difficult to distinguish—repeat important numbers in the center of the document or in words.

To improve the clarity of color catalog sheets or brochure pages, photocopy the material on a light setting before faxing. Remember, also, that standard writing paper in Europe is a different size than standard U.S. paper. European paper (called A-4) is longer and narrower—approximately 8"x11³/₄". As a result, avoid running material to the edge of a document.

❑ **Don't Abbreviate**

Because abbreviations are peculiar to each culture, avoid them whenever possible. When their use is dictated by space considerations, be sure to explain their meaning at some place in the document. A few common abbreviations differ radically between foreign countries and the United States. Take dates. In America, the day of June 11, 1997, is abbreviated 6/11/97. In Europe, the day comes before the month— 11/6/97. To avoid confusion, write out dates and use the European style whenever possible—with the day preceding the month and year: 11 June 1997.

❑ **Numbers: Their Commas and Periods**

American and British tradition call for commas to separate thousands in long number strings and a period to designate decimal fractions or to separate dollars from cents or pounds from pence. Europeans do just the reverse. A measurement of 1,067.52 in the United States becomes 1067,52 in Europe; £4,350.50 in England would be written as FM 4350,50 in Finland.

❑ **Netiquette**

While some Americans have adopted certain symbols to express emotions in E-Mail communications—":)" to show happiness; ":(" for sadness—these are not yet widely known abroad. Until they are, use *words* to convey feelings.

Measuring With Metrics

Basic Metric	~US Equivalent	Basic US	Metro Equivalent
1 centimeter (cm)	~3/8 inch	1 inch	2.54 cm
1 meter (m)	~ 1 yard	1 yard	91.44 cm
1 kilometer (km)	~5/8 mile	1 mile	1.6 km
1 square meter (m²)	~10 square feet	1 square foot	929.03 cm²
1 hectare (10,000m²)	~2.5 acres	1 acre	4,046.00 m²
1 gram (g)	~1/28 ounce (oz.)	1 oz.	28.35 g
1 kilogram (kg))	~2 pounds`	1 lb.	.45 kg
1000 kilograms	~ 1 ton	1 ton	980.00 kg
1 liter (l)	~ 2 pints	1 gallon	3.79 liters
-20° C	~0° F	1 ° F	.47° C
-10° C	~10° F	10° F	-12.0° C
0° C	32° F	20° F	-6.7° C
10° C	50° F	30° F	-1.1° C
20° C	~70° F	40° F	4.4° C
30° C	~85° F	50° F	10.0° C

Approximate Conversion Techniques

Inches:Centimeters	Double the inches and add 1/2 of them again to have an approximate metric length. For example, a 44" chest would measure approximately 110 cm. [44 x 2 + 22 = 110]
Miles:Kilometers	Muiltiply the number of miles by 8, then divide by 5. For example, 10 miles is equal to 16 kilometers [10 x 8 = 80; 80/5 = 16]
Square Feet:Square Meters	Divide number of square feet by 10. For example, a 180-square-foot office measures approximately 18 square meters. [100 / 10 = 18]
Ounces:Grams	Muiltiply the number of ounces by 30 to have an approximate idea of grams or if converting grams to ounces, simply divide by 30. For example, a 10 oz. bar of gold is equal to about 300 grams; a piece of jewelry containing 15 grams of gold has about 1/2 oz. [10 x 30 = 300; 15/30 = .5 or 1/2]
Pounds:Kilos	Divide the weight in half and subtract 10% of the result to get a metric equivalent. For example, a 100 pound woman weights 45 kilograms. [100 / 2 = 50; 50 x 10% = 5; 50 - 5 = 45]
Gallons:Liters	Multiply the gallons by 4, then subtract 5% of the result to determine number of liters. For example, 8 gallons is about 30 liters. [8 x 4 = 32; 32 x 5% = 1.6; 32 - 1.6 = 30.4]
Fahrenheit:Celsius	Deduct 32 from the Fahrenheit temperature, then divide in half for an approximate metric equivalent. To turn a Celsius temperature into an approximate Fahrenheit number, double the Celsius temperature and add 32. For example, 60°F is approximately 14° C; a 7° C reading is about 46° F. [60° F -32 = 28; 28 / 2 = 14°C] [7° C x 2 = 14; 14 + 32 =46°F]

Clothing Sizes

Remember that clothing sizes on the Continent employ a different system than found in Great Britain and both are different again from the system used in the United States. Take these differences into account when sending gifts to friends and colleagues abroad.

	SUITS	COLLARS	DRESSES/SKIRTS	SHOES
U.S. Men	36 38 40 42 44	15 15^1/2 16 16^1/2 17	-- -- -- -- -- --	7 8 9 10 11
U.S. Women	-- -- -- -- --	-- -- -- -- --	8 10 12 14 16	7^1/2 8^1/2 9^1/2 10^1/2 11^1/2
Cont. Europe	46 48 50 52 54	38 39^1/2 41 42 43	38 40 42 44 47	39 40^1/2 42 43 44^1/2
U.K.	36 38 40 42 44	15 15^1/2 16 16^1/2 17	10 12 14 16 18	6 7 8 9 10

Tipping

While American establishments rely on the customer to do the necessary tipping calculations at restaurants and bars, many countries in Europe *include* the service fee with a bill. If it is, these establishments usually add 15% to 18% of the value of the food and drink consumed and generally no further tip is required unless to reward extraordinary service. If service has not been added to a bill, customers are expected to add a tip in the 12% to 15% range.

When calculating tips for European services or rewarding people for assistance not related to a *monetary* amount, follow these general rules:

Baggage Give the local currency equivalent of $1.00 to $1.50 per bag—£1 in GB; DM 2.50 in Germany; FF 7.50 in France; L 2000 in Italy.

Taxis As a general rule, taxi drivers receive approximately 10% to 15% of the fare rounded up to the nearest convenient amount in the local currency. Thus a BEF 210 metered fare might be rounded to BEF 250.

Guides The local currency equivalent of about $1.00/hour/person in your party. For example, give the guide £ 2 for a two and one-half hour tour of London or DM 5 for a similar tour of Berlin.

Services For miscellaneous services (telephone operators, translators, concierge assistance), tip on the basis of the total amount of *time* involved in assisting you. Give the local currency equivalent—in round numbers—of approximately $5 for the first hour and $3 for each hour thereafter.

Currency Conversion

Pending the introduction of Euro notes in 2002, citizens of the European Union and tourists from outside of its boundaries will continue to have to deal with the daily challenge of finding the best rate and method of converting one currency into another.

The Editors of the *European Union Almanac* conducted an informal study of the rates and commissions involved in exchanging U.S. dollar cash—and dollar-denominated traveler's checks and credit cards—to British pounds on the same day. We discovered that while advertised *rates* may appear attractive, fees, fixed commissions, and other costs charged by different exchange facilities can alter the *effective* rate of the exchange received. We also found that the charge for exchanging traveler's checks is about 1 per cent *more* than for changing cash, but that using any credit card can mean a savings of as much as 20 per cent over using cash. We also learned some other details:

- Commissions can significantly alter the actual rate received for in-person exchanges of less than $100. While commissions are expressed as a percentage, there is usually a minimum amount for the first $100 exchanged. In other words, a 3 per cent commission when converting $20 or $100 can cost exactly the same amount—$3.00. But $3.00 taken out of a $20 bill amounts to an effective commission of 15 per cent!

- Most posted rates at exchange offices, in hotels, or at banks are far less than the rate printed in newspapers. The newspaper rates are for very large single transactions—usually for $1 million or more.

- Because the major credit card companies are buying and selling currencies on a daily basis in significant amounts, they are translating foreign currency transactions into the currency of their card holders' accounts at rates approaching those quoted in the newspaper.

As an example of the advantage of credit cards, the value of the pound officially closed in London on December 13, 1995 at $1.5325. A $100 conversion done at two different exchange houses that day—when the posted dollar buying rate outside was $1.56 to $1.58 for £1—actually was closer to $1.63 to $1.70 per £1 after costs. (Two $20 cash transactions we effected had the pound costing $1.83 at one facility and $1.95 at another.) Yet on credit card transactions that same day, even in amounts less than $20, American Express exchanged at $1.5555, Bank of America at $1.5563, and Citibank of New York at $1.5575.

ENGLISH	DANISH	DUTCH	FRENCH	GERMAN
Mr	Hr.	Dhr.	M.	H.
Mrs	Fru	Mevr.	Mme	Fr.
Ms	Fr.	—	Mme	Fr.
Miss	Frk.	Juffr.	Melle	Fr.
Hon.	—	—	Honorable	H
Dr	Dr.	Dr.	Dr	Dr.
Rev.	Pastor	Erwaarde	Révérend	Pfr.
Dean	—	Dir.	Doyen	Dek.
Prof.	Prof.	Prof.	Pr	Prof.
Gen.	Gen.	Gen.	G^{al}	Gen.
Adm.	Adm.	Adm.	Amiral	Adm.
Col.	Ob.	Kol.	Col.	Oberst
Maj.	Maj.	Maj.	Cdt	Maj.
Capt.	Kptn.	Kapt.	C^{ne}	Hptm.
Lieut.	Løjt.	Lt.	L^t	Lts.
Ens.	—	Vaandrig	Enseigne de vaisseau	LtzS.
WO	—	Adj. o. off.	—	OStFw. (Army) Ow.StBtsm. (Navy)
Sgt.	Sgt.	Serg.	Sgt	Fw.
CPO	—	—	—	PUO
Cpl.	KP	Korp.	Cpl	Uffz
Pvt.	MG	Sold.	Soldat	Gefr.
King	Kong	Koning	Roi	König
Queen	Dronning	Koningin	Reine	Königin
Prince	Prins	Prins	Prince	Prinz
Princess	Prinsesse	Prinses	Princesse	Prinzessin

TITLES AND ABBREVIATIONS

ITALIAN	NORWEGIAN	PORTUGUESE	SPANISH	SWEDISH
Sig.	Hr.	Sr.	Sr.	Hr
Sig.ra	Fru	Sra.	Sra.	Fru
Sig.ra	Fr.	Sra.	Dã.	Fr
Sig.na	Frk.	Men.	Srta.	Frk
On.	Ærede	Exmo.	Hrble.	—
Dott.	Dr.	Dr.	Dr.	Dr
Rev.	Past.	Rev.	Rvdo.	—
—	Dekanus	Reitor	Dec.	—
Prof.	Prof.	Prof.	Prof.	Prof.
Gen.	Gen.	Gen.	Gral.	Gen
Amm.	Adm.	Alm.	Almte.	Am
Col.	Oberst	Cor.	Cor.	Öv
Magg.	Maj.	Maj.	Cdte.	Mj
Cap.	Kapt.	Cap.	Cap.	Kpt
Ten.	Ltn.	Ten.	Ten.	Lt
—	Fenrik	Alf.	Alf.	Fn
Uff.	WO	Sub-ten.	Brig.	—
Serg.	Sjt.	Sarg.	Sarg.	Sgt
—	—	Fur.	—	Fj
Cpl.	Korp.	Cabo	Cabo	Kpr
Priv.	Menig	Soldado raso	Soldado	Mg
Re	Kong	Rei	Rey	Kung
Regina	Dronning	Rainha	Reina	Drottning
Principe	Prins	Príncipe	Príncipe	Prins
Principessa	Prinsesse	Princesa	Princesa	Prinsessa

Forms of Address

When addressing communications to individuals abroad, be sure to replicate the courtesy titles and university degrees/organizational honors found on their business cards or as part of the signature block of their letter to you. When addressing communications in English to a foreign dignatary, we suggest using a "Mid-Atlantic" style which combines usage acceptable in both the United States and Great Britain. As a result, instead of the traditional close to Royalty of "I have the honour to be your most humble and obedient servant," we recommend "Yours Respectfully." Note also that a period is commonly used with *abbreviations* and *initials*, but not contractions. Thus, Esq. abbreviates Esquire, but Mr is a contraction of the full spelling of Mister.

Business People	*Addressee*	_____, Esq.
	Greeting	Dear Mr/Mrs/Miss/Ms Jones:
	Close	Sincerely yours,
Professionals	*Addressee*	Mr/Mrs/Miss/Ms_____ __, A.B (Chem), F.I.O.D.
	Greeting	Dear Mr/Mrs/Miss/Ms_____:
	Close	Sincerely yours,
Academics	*Addressee*	Professor _____
	Greeting	Dear Dr _____:
	Close	Sincerely yours,
Medical Specialists	*Addressee*	_____, M.D.
	Greeting	Dear Dr _____:
	Close	Sincerely yours,
Organizations	*Addressee*	Office/Bureau/Department/Agency of_____
	Greeting	Gentlemen:
	Close	Sincerely yours,
President	*Addressee*	Hon. _____
	Greeting	Excellency:
	Close	Respectfully,
Prime Minister/Premier	*Addressee*	Rt Hon. _____
	Greeting	Dear Prime Minister/Premier_____:
	Close	Respectfully,
Cabinet Ministers	*Addressee*	Rt Hon._____
	Greeting	Sir/Madam:
	Close	Respectfully,
Judges	*Addressee*	Judge_____
	Greeting	Your Honor:
	Close	Respectfully,
Ambassadors	*Addressee*	Hon._____
	Greeting	Excellency:
	Close	Respectfully,

Governors/Mayors	*Addressee*	Mayor/Governor_____
	Greeting	Sir/Madam
	Close	Respectfully,
Clergy	*Addressee*	His Holiness Pope _____
	Greeting	Your Holiness
	Close	Respectfully,
	Addressee	_____Cardinal_____
	Greeting	Your Eminience
	Close	Respectfully,
	Addressee	The Most Reverend_____(Bishop)
	Greeting	Your Excellency
	Close	Respectfully,
	Addressee	Right Reverend_____(Monsignor)
	Greeting	Right Reverend Monsignor
	Close	Respectfully,
	Addressee	Reverend_____(Priest)
	Greeting	Dear Father_____:
	Close	Respectfully,
Royalty	*Addressee*	Emperor_____
	Greeting	Your Imperial Majesty
	Close	Yours Respectfully,
	Addressee	His Majesty_____
		King of _____
	Greeting	Your Majesty
	Close	Yours Respectfully,
	Addressee	Her Majesty_____
		Queen of _____
	Greeting	Your Majesty
	Close	Yours Respectfully,
	Addressee	His/Her Royal Highness (Prince/Princess)
	Greeting	Your Royal Highness
	Close	Yours Respectfully,
	Addressee	Duke/Duchess_____
	Greeting	Your Grace
	Close	Yours Respectfully,
	Addressee	Lord/Lady_____
	Greeting	My Lord/Lady
	Close	Yours Respectfully,

Taken from *World Almanac 1994* (Funk & Wagnalls), Judith Martin, *Miss Manners*, (Pharos Books) 1989, Adriana Hunter, *Etiquette* (HarperCollins), 1994, and Basildon Bond, *Letters for Every Occasion*, (W. Foulsham & Co., Ltd.), 1984.

Styling Mailing Addresses

Every country has a different tradition for preparing postal addresses. In some countries, the name of the country is put at the *top* of the address; in others, country designations appear as the *bottom line* of an address. In many places the number of a building is put *before* the street name; in others, the street name is noted first, the number *afterwards*. Postal codes have enormous differences—a letter and 4 numbers in Austria; 3 and 4 digit number and letter combinations separated into two groups in Great Britain —as well as different locations within a written address block.

To achieve some uniformity, we recommend that the traditions of both the sender's and recipient's postal authorities be honored when addressing items to be sent through the mails. For example, when addressing a letter in another language or alphabet (for Greek or Russian, for example), put the individual's name as well as the city and country name in Roman letters at the bottom of the address—even if it represents duplicate information. Here is an example of how to address a letter to a country that is neither in the EU nor uses the Roman alphabet:

РОССИЯ	Name of country
117977 Москва, В-334	6 Digit Postal Code and Moscow regional code
ул.Косыгина, д.4,	Street Address
Институт химической физики РАН	Name of Institution—on two lines
Проф. ИВАНОВУ А. П.	Individual addressee
Prof. A. P. Ivanov	Addressee—Repeated in English
(Moscow) RUSSIA	City and County—Repeated in English

Since local postal officials are responsible for moving mail abroad, print the city and country destination at the end of an address block where they are accustomed to looking for it. But then follow the foreign country's format to assist the foreign postal authorities in making final delivery of the letter or parcel.

Because country of origin is not always clear from city names, regional abbreviations, postal codes, or even metered imprints or postage stamps, always try to remember to spell out the state name (very few sources readily available abroad list U.S. postal abbreviations) and be sure to add the letters USA on all return addresses

The Americas Group
9200 Sunset Blvd., Suite 404
Los Angeles, California 90069
USA

European Delivery Data

Ordinary first class mail to a major European gateway city generally takes 4 business days—a letter posted on Monday should reach its destination by Friday; a letter mailed on Wednesday should arrive on the following Monday Add two to three days for Small Package deliveries. If a letter or small parcel is destined for a smaller town outside of a major gateway city, allow one more day for internal transportation, sorting, and delivery.

US Postal Service	First Class	Small Package (Air)
$^1/_2$ oz.	$.60	--.--
1 oz.	$1.00	$.90
1 $^1/_2$ oz.	$1.40	--.--
2 oz.	$1.80	$1.32
2 $^1/_2$ oz.	$1.40	--.--
3 oz.	$1.80	$1.74
3 $^1/_2$ oz.	$2.20	--.--
4 oz.	$2.60	$2.16
4 $^1/_2$ oz.	$3.00	--.--
5 oz.	$3.40	--.--
5 $^1/_2$ oz.	$3.80	--.--
6 oz.	$4.20	$3.00
6 $^1/_2$ oz.	$4.60	--.--
7 oz.	$5.00	--.--
7 $^1/_2$ oz.	$5.40	--.--
8 oz.	$5.80	$3.84
1 lb.	$13.00	$7.20
1$^1/_2$ lb.	$19.40	$9.60
2 lb.	$35.80	$14.40
3 lb.	$27.40	$16.80

International courier service to major European cities takes two business days. A small package picked up by or delivered to FedEx, DHL, UPS, U.S. Postal Service, or Airborne Express on Monday, will reach its European destination on Wednesday; a package sent on Wednesday can be expected to be in the hands of its intended recipient by Friday. Prices on small packages vary with weight and destination. An 8 oz. envelope, dropped off at an office or in a bin, runs between $26 and $29 to European Union countries; DHL will pick up the same package for $27 to $36. UPS handles up to 1 lb. for $25—for Western European destinations—and $29 for Central European countries. These prices can also vary with special promotions and incentive programs.

Styling Names

If determining the gender of a person is sometimes difficult for Americans, it can be nearly impossible for foreigners. Take the following list. Would you guess these to be the given names of men or women—or both—in the United States:

Adrian	*Gale*
Beverly	*Jamie*
Bobby	*Leslie*
Dana	*Michael*
Darrell	*Robin*
Fran	*Sydney*

How about the gender of people in other cultures with the following given names:

Gesche
Janne
Mazie
Vivian

As a matter of courtesy and clarity in international communications, insert a gender indicator in all *initial* written contacts. For example, the editors of this book might use the following signature block the first time either sends a communication to someone abroad:

```
Sincerely yours,          With best wishes,

(Mr) Godfrey Harris       (Mrs) Adelheid Hasenknopf
```

Finally, beware of addressing foreigners in written communications by their given names without being invited to do so. People in other cultures tend to be more formal than Americans and the use of nicknames may only be appropriate in oral communication. While some will invite you to call them by their given names, most will offer signals within documents to indicate when a relationship has moved to a more intimate stage. Watch signatures on documents or references within documents for the appropriate signals. If unsure, always ask.

Asking is also imperative when dealing with the transliterations of Chinese, Korean, and other Oriental names. Many of these place the family name first and the given name afterwards. Some, however, anticipate confusion among Westerners and reverse the order of their names. If unsure, always ask.

Styling Telephone Numbers

Telephone numbers appearing on stationery and business cards should be printed with international communications in mind. Because 800 numbers are not normally accessible from abroad, always be sure to provide a local telephone number on all brochures, instruction manuals, and other printed material.

While by no means uniform as yet, many businesses today use the "+" sign to indicate the use of the international direct dial access number, parenthesis around the country code, with no dashes or other punctuation used to designate or separate the regional code and the subscriber's number. For example, the telephone number of the publishers of this book is displayed for international communications as follows:

+ (1) 310 278 8038

Indicates local numbers that must be dialed for direct access to international telephone service.

See page 49 for the access numbers used in EU countries.

This is the country code. It can be one, two or three digits (see page 49 for EU codes.)

For example, the code (1) is used from anywhere in the world to direct dial telephone numbers located in the United States, Canada, and the Caribbean.

This is called an area code in the United States and corresponds to a specific geographic region. In Europe, area codes are called city codes and often coincide with a particular political jurisdiction.

City codes in the EU, when required, are 1 to 4 digits. Many phone numbers also show an initial "0" as part of the city code. This number is *only* used when making an internal long distance call and can usually be ignored when dialing internationally.

While most countries are now using 7 digit numbers for individual telephone subscribers, there are still wide differences on how the numbers should be grouped for display. When quoting 7 digit numbers, use a 3 number and 4 number pattern as above. Divide six digits into three groups of two—as in 25 80 21.

A few areas have moved to 8 digit subscriber telephone numbers. Separate this longer sequence into four groups of 2 digits each to facilitate understanding and remembering.

Some 9 digit subscriber lines also now exist. When referring to them, divide them into 3 groups of three digits each.

Answering Machines

Be conscious that direct dialing capability from anywhere in the world has generated two problems. Some foreign phone systems do not emit the same tones as American phones. As a result, people using these systems cannot follow menu prompts. In addition, many phone users are not fluent in English. To solve both problems, we recommend that a separate line be dedicated to incoming foreign language callers. The message on the answering machine would offer instructions in several different languages and would not require any action on the part of the foreign caller other than to leave a message concerning their order or their needs.

Guidelines for Foreign Language Translations

Sometimes, of course, written communication in English is totally inappropriate—in advertising copy, supply catalogs, and instruction material to name just a few instances. At other times, documents originating in a foreign language must be rendered accurately into English to ensure complete understanding of legal obligations and financial commitments. At such times, selecting an appropriate translator requires a review of the following five issues:

- Is the language to be translated the mother tongue of the individual who will do the work? Is the translator a member of a professional organization and/or is he or she licensed by an official agency?

- What is the substantive field of specialty of the translator (business, finance, law, engineering, literature, etc.) and what type of experience as a translator does the individual bring to the task at hand?

- What methodology will the translator use for this job—the entire job by one person, partially or wholly computer assisted, with or without client discussions of ambiguous elements of the original?

- How will the finished product be presented and in how many copies—by hand, by electronic media, by disk?

- What will be the cost of the job be and how long will it take to complete?

Translation is not generally a word-for-word rendering from one language to another; rather, translation requires the practitioner to convey the author's original meaning—in the full sense of that term—as accurately as possible. While translations are often treated as a task for anyone who may *speak* another language—with all the perils inherent when inappropriate, embarrassing, and sometimes costly mistakes are made—they are today an integral part of international business and an essential element in understanding those who live across linguistic boundaries.

Based on an interview with Trade Translation & Services of London and Godfrey Harris and Charles Sonabend, *Commercial Translations* (The Americas Group), 1985.

Value Added Tax

The Value Added Tax (VAT) is universal in Europe. While similar to sales taxes found in the United States, a sales tax is only applied at the point of consumption. Value Added taxes, on the other hand, are added at *every* stage of the production or development of all goods and services in the economy—from their inception to their consumption. VAT taxes vary from country to country, but are generally in the 15% to 19% range.

Foreign visitors are usually eligible to receive VAT rebates for certain expenditures made abroad:

- Lodging
- Sustenance
- Ground transportation
- Exhibit costs
- Professional fees
- Car rentals
- Training courses
- Retail purchases

As a general rule, rebates are awarded on the basis of receipts. Receipts should show the name and address of the service provider; the name of the individual receiving the service and his or her company's name; the date and nature of the transaction; and the VAT rate charged for the transaction. Large amounts—amounts in excess of £100 or DM 200—should specify the VAT percentage rate involved *as well as* the amount charged.

Since each country has its own specific rules on what additional information may be required before a refund is paid and every country has its own time limits and forms for handling VAT rebates, many individuals have come to rely on specialist companies to process their VAT rebates. These companies charge a commission on the amount recovered; some charge nothing if no rebate is issued.

For more information on VAT services from one of these companies, contact either:

Vatback International
Eurotax Reclaim Service
17610 Midway Road—#134
Dallas, Texas 75287
USA
+ (1) 214 407 7537

Quipsound
European VAT Recovery
The Crown Building, London Road
Westerham, Kent TN16 1DP
ENGLAND
+ (44) 1959 56 47 40

Diacritical Marks and Special Letters

Very few words used in English language communication carry diacritical marks—résumé, naïve, and mañana come to mind as do José and Álvaro; more importantly, the lack of their use is generally not significant to understanding. In foreign languages, however, diacritical marks can be crucial to usage and pronunciation. When a foreign name or word carries a diacritical mark, learn how to reproduce them on your computer, word processor, or typewriter.

MARK	MACINTOSH (APPLE) STROKES (MICROSOFT WORD)	IBM STROKES (WORDPERFECT)
À, È, Ì, Ò, Ù à, è, ì, ò, ù	Option Key and Grave Key " ` " (next to number 1 on keyboard), then letter to be accented. For capital letter, use Shift key before striking letter to be accented.	To make Diacritical marks, use Printer's characters when available by inserting a Printer Escape Code where you want character is to appear.
Å, å	Option Key and letter "a". For a capital letter, use the Shift Key.	When foreign characters are not supported by the printer, use Overstrike to create them.
Á, É, Í, Ó, Ú á, é, í, ó, ú	Option Key and letter "e" (nothing will show on screen), then letter to be accented. For capital letters with these marks, click on the All Caps box in the Character window under the Format menu.	To create an Overstrike, move cursor to the point two (or more) characters are wanted in the same place. Then press Format (Shift/F8), chose Other, chose Overstrike, and create. Enter the Characters wanted, press Enter, then Exit (F8) to return to document.
Ä, Ë, Ï, Ö, Ü ä, ë, ï, ö, ü	Option key and letter "u", then letter to be accented. Make lower case letter with accent (as above), then highlight to change to a capital letter using the Character window under the Format menu.	
Â, Ê, Î, Ô, Û â, ê, î, ô, û	Option key and letter "i", then letter to be accented. For a capital letter, use the Shift Key.	Note: Even though Overstrike strokes will appear in your document, only the last character entered will appear on the screen.
Ñ, ñ	Option key and letter "n", then letter to be accented. For a capital letter, use the Shift Key.	
Ø, ø	Option key and letter "o". For capital letters, click on the All Caps box in the Character window under the Format menu.	
Æ, æ	Option key and foot symbol " ' " (next to Return on keyboard). For capital letters, click on the All Caps box in the Character window under the Format menu.	
ß	Used in place of "ss;" but never use three "s's" in a row when substituting ß for ss.	

TITLES IN INTERNATIONAL BUSINESS

FOREWORD

In business, a title can have many practical functions. It provides information on a person's area of responsibility, function and authority. However, its significance is not only practical. For many people, the title forms part of their identity, and thus part of their personality.

To help ensure successful international communication, everyone involved in international business must have reliable information about titles in other countries. Each country has its own national customs, and individual companies and institutions have their own traditions in giving titles to employees.

This section, which is a pioneering work in its field, is the result of comprehensive research by philologists and translators from numerous European countries. It contains a selection of titles most frequently used in the international business world in the 10 most important European languages.

This section offers readers an important communication tool for international business relations. We wish those who use it every success in their work.

Gunnar Lindberg
Swedish Trade Council
Translation and Interpreting Services

Mr Lindberg heads Translation and Interpreting Services, a wholly-owned subsidiary of the Swedish Trade Council. Prior to assuming this position, Mr Lindberg served as Director of Marketing for the Swedish Trade Council's Institute of Export and then established an editing and publishing service for the Council. He holds an MBA from the University of Uppsala and is fluent in Swedish, English, German, and French.

Sverre Særen
Norwegian Trade Council
International Assignment Services

Mr Særen is a graduate of the Oslo School of Economics and has been employed by the Norwegian Trade Council since 1991. As Director of International Assignment Services, Mr Særen provides training programs for employees of Norwegian companies and government agencies posted abroad. Between 1976 and 1989, Mr Særen worked for the American construction firm of Brown & Root.

USER GUIDE

European equivalents of American titles are listed in the opening portion of this section. Where a British title differs from an American title, the British title is shown in brackets below the American title.

A Cross Reference Titles Index follows the translations of American titles. In this index, readers will find an alphabetical listing of all titles as they appear in nine foreign languages. In the case of British titles, the Cross Reference Titles Index lists only those that are different from their American equivalents.

Because of different corporate and administrative structures in various linguistic areas, exact translations are not always available. When this occurs, the nearest equivalent is given. Some languages have different masculine and feminine forms of various titles. To make the presentation clearer here, masculine forms only are used.

Broadly speaking, the titles appear in both the private and public sectors. Where there are differences in public and private sector usage, explanations appear in parenthesis.

New titles come into being and others rapidly go out-of-date; new facts appear to supercede others. The editors will therefore be grateful for comments and suggestions for new titles as well as categories of information for future editions of this book.

Adelheid Hasenknopf
European Editor

Godfrey Harris
American Editor

ENGLISH	DANISH	DUTCH	FRENCH	GERMAN
Accountant	Bogholder	Boekhouder	Compatable	Buchhalter
Actuary	Aktuar	Actuaris	Actuaire	Aktuar
Administrative Manager	Administrationsleder Administrativ chef Forvaltningschef	Hoofd administratieafdeling	Responsable administratif	Verwaltungsdirektor
Advertising Manager/ Director	Reklamechef	Hoofd publiciteit Hoofd reclame	Directeur de la publicité Directeur du service publicité Responsable de la publicité	Leiter der Werbeabteilung
Agent	Agent	Agent Vertegenwoordiger	Agent	Agent Vertreter
Ambassador	Ambassadør	Ambassadeur	Ambassadeur	Botschafter
Architect	Arkitekt	Architect	Architecte	Architekt
Assistant	Assistent	Assistent	Adjoint Assistant	Assistent
Assistant ...	Medhjælpende ...	Adjunct-... Plaatsvervangend...	... adjoint ... délégué ... suppléant	...assistent Stellvertretender ...
Assistant Director	Vicedirektør	Adjunct-directeur	Secrétaire d'administration	Stellvertrender Direktor
Assistant Marketing Manager	Marketingassistent	Assistent marketing	Assistant marketing	Assistent der Marketingleitung

ITALIAN	NORWEGIAN	PORTUGUESE	SPANISH	SWEDISH
Contabile	Revisor	Contabilista	Contador	Revisor
Attuario	Aktuar	Actuário	Actuario	Aktuarie
Capo servizi amministrativi	Administra-sjonssjef	Chefe administrativo	Jefe Administrativo	Administrativ chef
	Forvaltningssjef			Förvaltningschef
Direttore servizi pubblicità	Reklamesjef	Chefe de publicidade	Jefe Publicidad	Reklamchef
			Director de Publicidad	
Agente	Agent	Agente	Agente	Agent
			Delegado	
			Representante	
Ambasciatore	Ambassadør	Embaixador	Embajador	Ambassadör
Architetto	Arkitekt	Arquitecto	Arquitecto	Arkitekt
Assistente	Assistent	Assistente	Asistente	Assistent
			Auxiliar	
			Ayudante del...	
... aggiunto	Assisterende ...	... adjunto	... Adjunto	Biträdande
Vice...	Vise...	... assistente		
		... auxiliar		
Direttore aggiunto	Assisterende direktør	Vice-Director	Director (de ...)	Direktör-assistent
Vicedirettore			Director de(l) Departamento	
Assistente al marketing	Markedsassistent	Assistente de marketing	Asistente de Marketing	Marknads-assistent

ENGLISH	DANISH	DUTCH	FRENCH	GERMAN
Auditor	Revisor	Accountant Revisor	Audit	Revisor Wirtschaftprüfer
Bank Director	Bankdirektør	Bankdirecteur	Directeur de banque	Bankdirektor
Bank Manager	Bankdirektør	Bankdirecteur	Directeur de banque	Bankdirektor
Branch Manager	Filialchef Filialleder	Filiaalhouder	Directeur de succursale	Filialleiter/ direktor Zweigstellenleiter
Broker	Mægler	Makelaar	Courtier	Makler
Building ...	Bygnings...	Bouw...	... du bâtiment	Bau...
Buyer	Indkøber	Inkoper	Acheteur	Einkäufer
Chairman of the Board (of Directors)	Bestyrelses-formand	Voorzitter van de raad van beheer	Président du conseil d'administration	Aufsichtsrats-vorsitzender Verwaltungs-ratsvorsitzender Vorstandsvor-sitzender
Chairman/person	Formand	President Voorzitter	Président	Präsident Vorsitzender
Chief ...	Chef	Chef Hoofd	Chef Directeur	Chef Leiter
Chief Accountant	Hovedbogholder	Hoofdboekhouder	Chef comptable	Oberbuchhalter
Chief Editor	Chefredaktør	Hoofdredacteur	Rédacteur en chef	Chefredakteur

ITALIAN	NORWEGIAN	PORTUGUESE	SPANISH	SWEDISH
Revisore	Revisor	Auditor	Auditor	Revisor
		Revisor de contas		
Direttore di banca	Bankdirektør	Gerente bancário	Director del Banco	Bankdirektör
Direttore di banca	Banksjef	Gerente bancário	Director del Banco	Bankdirektör
Direttore di filiale	Filialsjef	Chefe de sucursal	Director de Sucursal	Filialchef
				Platschef
Agente Intermediatore	Megler	Agente intermediário	Agente de Seguros	Mäklare
		Corretor	Corredor	
... edile	Bygge...	... de construção	... de Construcciones	Byggnads...
	Bygnings...		... de Obras	
Compratore	Innkjøper	Agente de compras	Comprador	Inköpare
		Comprador		
Presidente del consiglio di amministrazione	Styreformann	Presidente do Conselho de Administração	Presidente del Consejo de Administración	Styrelseordförande
Presidente	Ordfører	Presidente	Presidente	Ordförande
	Ordstyrer			
Capo	Sjef	Chefe	Jefe	Chef
Capo contabile	Regnskapssjef	Chefe de contabilidade	Jefe de Contabilidad	Ekonomichef
Redattore capo	Sjefredaktør	Redactor-chefe	Redactor en Jefe	Chefredaktör
			Redactor Jefe	

ENGLISH	DANISH	DUTCH	FRENCH	GERMAN
Chief Engineer	Overingeniør	Hoofdingenieur	Ingénieur en chef	Chefingenieur Leitender Ingenieur Oberingenieur
Chief Financial Officer	Økonomichef Økonomidirektør	Hoofd financiële afdeling	Administrateur financier Chef du service financier Directeur financier	Leiter der Finanzabteilung Leiter des Finanz- und Rechnungswesens
Chief of Police [Head of Police]	Politichef	Commissaris van politie	Chef du service local de police	Polizeipräsident
Chief of Security Section/ Department [Head of Security]	Sikkerhedschef	Hoofd veiligheids-dienst	Chef du service de sécurité	Wekschutzleiter
Chief of Staff [Head of Staff Section/ Department/ Division]	Personalechef Personaledirektør	Personeelschef	Chef du personnel Chef du service du personnel Directeur du personnel Directeur du service du personnel	Leiter/Direktor der Personal-abteilung Personalchef Personalleiter/ direktor
Chief Training Officer	Uddannelsesleder	Hoofd dienst opleiding	Chef de la formation Chef du service formation Directeur du service formation Responsable de la formation	Leiter der Schulungsab-teilung Leiter des Aus- und Forbildungs-wesens Schulungs-leiter
Chief/Head Buyer	Indkøbschef	Inkoopchef	Directeur des achats	Einkaufsleiter Leiter der Einkaufsab-teilung

ITALIAN	NORWEGIAN	PORTUGUESE	SPANISH	SWEDISH
Ingegnere capo	Overingeniør	Engenheiro-chefe	Ingeniero Jefe	Överingenjör
Capo del servizio finanziario	Økonomidirektør Økonomisjef	Director de departamento financeiro	Administrador de Finanzas	Ekonomichef Ekonomidirektör
Questore	Politimester	Chefe-Geral da Polícia	Jefe del Servicio Local de Policía	Polischef
Responsabile Sicurezza	Sikkerhetssjef	Chefe de segurança	Jefe del Servicio de Seguridad	Säkerhetschef
Capo del personale	Personaldirektør Personalsjef	Chefe de pessoal Chefe do departamento de pessoal	Jefe del Servicio de Personal	Personalchef Personaldirektör
Responsabile formazione	Opplæringssjef	Chefe do departamento de formação interna	Engargado de la Formación del Personal	Utbildningschef
Capo servizio acquisti	Innkjøpssjef	Chefe de compras	Jefe de Compras	Inköpschef

ENGLISH	DANISH	DUTCH	FRENCH	GERMAN
Chief/Senior/ Head Accountant	Hovedbogholder	Hoofdaccountant Hoofdboekhouder	Chef comptable	Leiter der Buchhaltung Oberbuchhalter
Commercial Representative	Repræsentant	Handelsvertegen-woordiger	Représentant de commerce	Handelsvertreter
Computer Manager	Datachef EDB-chef	Hoofd A.G.V. Hoofd automa-tische gegevens-verwerking Hoofd informatica-dienst	Directeur de l'informatique Directeur du service informatique	Leiter der EDV-Abteilung Leiter des Rechenzentrums
Consul	Konsul	Consul	Consul	Konsul
Consultant	Konsulent	Adviseur Raadsman	Conseil Conseiller Consultant	Berater
Contracts Manager	Kontraktchef	Hoofd contract-afdeling	Chef du service contrats Responsable des contrats	Leiter der Abteilung für Vertragsfragen
Copywriter	Copywriter	Copywriter	Concepteur-rédacteur	Werbetexter
Customs Director	Toldchef	Inspecteur general bij de douane	Directeur des douanes	Leiter/Direktor des Zollamts Leiter/Direktor der Zollstelle

ITALIAN	NORWEGIAN	PORTUGUESE	SPANISH	SWEDISH
Perito contabile	Regnskapssjef	Chefe de contabilidade	Jefe de Contabilidad	Kamrer Redovisnings-chef
Rappresentante	Representant Selger	Agente de vendas Representante	Agente Comercial	Representant
Capo dei servizi informatici Responsabile servizio EDP	Datasjef EDB-sjef	Chefe dos serviços de informática	Jefe del Servicio Informático	ADB-chef Datachef
Console	Konsul	Cônsul	Cónsul	Konsul
Consulente	Konsulent Rådgiver	Consultor	Consultor	Konsult
Responsabile delle commesse	Kontraktssjef	Chefe do departamento de contratos	Jefe de Contratos	Kontraktschef
Copy Creativo Redattore di testi pubblicitari	Tekstforfatter	Copy-Writer Redactor de textos de publicidade	Redactor Planificador	Copywriter
Direttore della dogana	Tollsjef	Chefe de alfândega	Director de Aduana Jefe de Aduana	Tullchef

ENGLISH	DANISH	DUTCH	FRENCH	GERMAN
Data Processing Manager	Datachef EBD-chef	Hoofd A.G.V. Hoofd automatische gegevensver- werking Hoofd informa- tieverwerking	Directeur de l'informatique Directeur du service informatique	Leiter der EDV- Abteilung Leiter des Rechenzen- trums
Dental Surgeon/ Dentist	Tandlæge	Tandarts	Chirurgien- dentiste	Zahnarzt
Departmental Manager	Afdelingschef	Afdelingshoofd	Chef de service	Abteilungsleiter Referatsleiter
Deputy ...	Medhjælpende ...	Adjunct...	... adjoint ... délégué	...assistent Stellvertretender ...
Deputy Chief of Mission [Head of Chancellery]	Sekretariatschef	Kanselarijhoofd	Chef de chancellerie	Kanzleivorsteher
Deputy Director	Vicedirektør	Afdelings- directeur	Sous-directeur (Public Admin.)	Stellvertretender Direktor
Deputy General Manager	Vice-general- direktør	Adjunct-alge- meendirecteur adjoint	Directeur général	Stellvertretender Generaldirektor
Deputy Marketing Manager	Marketingass- istent	Assistent marketing	Assistant de marketing	Assistent der Marketingleitung
Design Engineer	Konstruktør	Ontwerpingenieur	Ingénieur- projeteur	Konstrukteur
Development Engineer	Udviklingsin- geniør	Ontwikkelings- ingenieur	Ingénieur (de) développement	Entwicklungs- ingenieur
Development Manager	Udviklingschef	Hoofd ontwikkelings- afdeling	Chef du service développement Directeur du développement	Leiter der Entwicklungs- abteilung

ITALIAN	NORWEGIAN	PORTUGUESE	SPANISH	SWEDISH
Capo dei servizi informatici	Datasjef EDB-sjef	Chefe dos serviços de informática	Jefe del Servicio Informático	ADB-chef Datachef
Responsabile servizio EDP				
Dentista	Tannlege	Médico dentista	Dentista	Tandläkare
Capo reparto Capo sezione	Avdelingssjef	Chefe de secção	Jefe Departa- mental	Avdelningschef
Vice...	Assisterende ... Vise...	... adjunto ... assistente ... auxiliar	... Adjunto	Biträdande ...
Cancelliere capo	Byråsjef	Canceler	Canciller	Kanslichef
Vicedirettore	Underdirektør	Vice-Director	Director de(l) Departamento	Byrådirektör
Vicedirettore generale	Viseadministre- rende direktør	Vicegerente	Subdirector Vicegerente	Vice verkställande direktör
Assistente al marketing	Markedsassistent	Assistente de marketing	Director Adjunto de Comercialización	Marknads- assistent
Progettista	Konstruktør	Construtor	Ingeniero Proyectista	Konstruktör
Ingegnere di sviluppo Tecnico addetto allo sviluppo	Utviklingsingeniør	Engenheiro de desenvolvimento	Ingeniero de Desarrollo	Utvecklingsin- genjör
Responsabile sviluppo	Utviklingssjef	Chefe do departa- mento de desen- volvimento	Jefe del Departamento de Desarrollo	Utvecklingschef

ENGLISH	DANISH	DUTCH	FRENCH	GERMAN
Director	Direktør	Directeur	Directeur Directeur général Gérant	Direktor
Director of (the ...) Department ...	Afdelingsdirektør	Afdelings-directeur	Chef de service Directeur de service	Abteilungsleiter
Director of Administration [Head of Administration]	Administrativ di-rektør/leder/chef Forvaltningschef	Administratief directeur Hoofd administratie	Directeur administratif	Verwaltungs-direktor
Director of Customs	Toldchef	Inspecteur-general bij de douane	Directeur des douanes	Leiter/Direktor des Zollamts
Director of Export Section/ Department/ Division	Eksportdirektør	Directeur export-afdeling	Directeur des exportations Directeur du service (des) exportations	Leiter der Exportabteilung
Director of Finance	Økonomidirektør	Directeur financiële afdeling	Directeur financier	Leiter der Finanzabteilung
Director of Hospital Services	Sygehusdirektør	Ziekenhuisdirecteur	Directeur des hôpitaux	Krankenhaus-direktor
Director of Marketing	Marketingdirektør	Marketing directeur	Directeur du marketing	Marketingleiter
Director of Planning (Section/ Department/ Division)	Planlægnings-direktør	Hoofd plannings-afdeling	Directeur de la planification Directeur du Service de planification	Leiter/Direktor der Planungsabtei-lung

ITALIAN	NORWEGIAN	PORTUGUESE	SPANISH	SWEDISH
Direttore	Direktør	Director	Director	Direktör
Direttore del reparto	Avdelingsdirektør	Director de secção	Director del Departamento de ...	Avdelnings-direktör
Direttore amministrativo	Administrasjons-sjef	Director /Chefe administrativo	Director/Jefe Administrativo	Administrativ direktör
Capo servizi amministrativi	Forvaltningssjef			Förvaltningschef
Direttore della dogana	Tollsjef	Director de alfândega	Director de Aduana	Tullchef
Direttore servizio esportazione	Eksportsjef	Director de exportações	Director de Exportación	Exportdirektör
Direttore finanziario	Økonomidirektør	Director de departamento financeiro	Director Financiero	Ekonomidirektör
Direttore d'ospedale	Sykehusdirektør	Director de hospital	Director de Centro Hospitalario Director de Hospitales	Sjukhusdirektör
Direttore del marketing	Markedsdirektør	Director do departamento de marketing	Director de Marketing	Marknadsdirek-tör
Direttore della pianificazione	Planleggings-direktør	Director de planeamento	Director de Planificación	Planerings-direktör

ENGLISH	DANISH	DUTCH	FRENCH	GERMAN
Director of Public Relations	Informations-direktør	Directeur informatiedienst Directeur PR-afdeling	Directeur des relations extérieures Directeur des relations publiques Directeur du service information	Direktor der Abteilung für Öffentlich-keitsarbeit PR-Direktor
Director of Research	Forskningschef Forskningsleder	Directeur onderzoeksaf-deling	Directeur de la recherche	Leiter der Forschungs-abteilung
Director of Sales (Market-ing) (Section/ Department/ Division)	Salgsdirektør	Verkoop-directeur	Directeur commercial Directeur des ventes Directeur du service des ventes	Verkaufsleiter
Director-General (D.-G.)	Generaldirektør	Algemeen directeur Directeur-generaal	Directeur général	Generaldirektor
Distribution Director	Salgsdirektør	Distributiedirecteur	Directeur commercial Directeur des ventes Directeur du service des ventes	Vertriebsleiter

ITALIAN	NORWEGIAN	PORTUGUESE	SPANISH	SWEDISH
Direttore servizio informazioni	Informasjons-direktør	Director de informação	Director de Relaciones Públicas	Informations-direktör
Direttore della ricerca	Forskningssjef	Director do departamento de investigação	Director de Investigación	Forskningschef
Direttore servizio vendite	Salgsdirektør	Director do departamento de ventas	Director de Ventas	Försäljnings-direktör
Direttore generale	Generaldirektør	Director -Geral	Director General	Generaldirektör
Direttore della distribuzione	Salgsdirektør	Director do departamento de vendas	Director de Ventas	Försäljnings-direktör

ENGLISH	DANISH	DUTCH	FRENCH	GERMAN
Distribution Manager	Distributionschef Salgschef	Hoofd distributie Verkoopchef	Chef de la distribution Chef des ventes Chef du service des ventes Directeur de la distribution Directeur des ventes Directeur du service des ventes	Verkaufsleiter/ direktor Vertriebsleiter/ direktor
District Manager	Distriktschef	Districtshoofd	Directeur régional	Bezirksleiter Gebietsleiter
Divisional Director	Divisionschef/ direktør	Divisiedirecteur	Chef de département Chef de division	Divisions- direktor
Divisional Head	Divisionschef	Divisiedirecteur	Chef de département Chef de division	Geschäftsbe- reichsleiter
Divisional Manager	Divisionschef	Hoofd divisie	Chef de département Chef de division	Geschäftsbe- reichsleiter
Drafting Office Manager [Drawing Office Manager]	Konstruktions- chef Tegnestueleder	Hoofd ontwikke- lingsafdeling	Chef du bureau d'études Concepteur-pro- jecteur en chef Directeur du bureau d'études	Chefkonstruk- teur Konstruktions- leiter Leiter der Konstruktions- abteilung
Editor-in-Chief	Chefredaktør	Hoofdredacteur	Rédacteur en chef	Chefredakteur
... Engineer	Ingeniør	Ingenieur	Ingénieur	Ingenieur

ITALIAN	NORWEGIAN	PORTUGUESE	SPANISH	SWEDISH
Capo distribuzione Capo servizio distribuzione	Distribusjonssjef Salgssjef	Chefe de distribuição	Jefe de Ventas	Försäljningschef Distributionschef
Capo distretto	Distriktssjef	Chefe regional	Director Regional	Distriktschef
Direttore di divisione	Divisjonssjef	Chefe de divisão	Jefe de División	Divisionschef
Capo divisione	Divisjonssjef	Chefe de divisão	Jefe de División	Divisionschef
Capo divisione	Divisjonssjef	Chefe de divisão	Jefe de División	Divisionschef
Capo dell'ufficio di progettazione	Konstruksjonssjef	Chefe de construção	Jefe del Gabinete de Estudios Jefe del Gabinete de Proyectos	Konstruktions-chef
Redattore capo	Sjefredaktør	Redactor-chefe	Redactor Jefe	Chefredaktör
Ingegnere Tecnico	Ingeniør	Engenheiro	Ingeniero	Ingenjör

ENGLISH	DANISH	DUTCH	FRENCH	GERMAN
Executive Assistant [Senior (Managing/ Signing/ Confidential) Clerk]	Prokurist	Gevolmachtigde Procuratiehouder	Fondé de pouvoir	Prokurist
Export Director	Eksportdirektør	Directeur export-afdeling	Directeur des exportations Directeur du service (des) exportations	Direktor der Exportabteilung
Export Manager	Eksportchef	Hoofd export-afdeling	Chef des exportations Chef du service (des) exportations Directeur des exportations	Leiter der Exportabteilung
Factory Manager [Works Manager]	Fabrikschef Fabriksleder	Fabrieksdirecteur	Gérant Directeur d'usine	Fabrikdirektor Werksdirektor Werksleiter
Financial Manager	Økonomichef Finanschef	Hoofd financiële afdeling	Administrateur financier Chef du service financier Directeur du service financier Directeur financier	Leiter der Finanzabteilung Leiter des Finanz- und Rechnungs-wesens Leiter/Direktor der Finanzab-teilung
Fire Marshal [Chief Fire Officer]	Brandsikkerheds-chef	Diensthoofd brand-bestrijding	Chef des services de lutte contre l'incendie	Brandschutzleiter

ITALIAN	NORWEGIAN	PORTUGUESE	SPANISH	SWEDISH
Procuratore	Prokurist	Procurador	Apoderado	Prokurist
Direttore vendite esportazione	Eksportdirektør	Director de exportações	Director del Servicio Exportaciones	Exportdirektör
Capo ufficio vendite esportazione	Eksportsjef	Chefe de exportações	Jefe de Exportación	Exportchef
Capo fabbrica	Fabrikksjef Verkssjef	Chefe de fábrica	Director de la Fábrica	Disponent Fabrikschef Verkschef
Responsabile finanziario	Økonomisjef Finanssjef	Gestor financeiro	Administrador de Finanzas	Ekonomichef Finanschef
Comandante dei vigili del Fuoco	Brannsjef	Chefe de serviço de luta contra os incêndios	Jefe del Servicio Antiincendio	Brandchef

ENGLISH	DANISH	DUTCH	FRENCH	GERMAN
Foreman	Arbejdsleder	Ploegbaas	Agent de maîtrise	Bauleiter
		Voorman	Chef d'atelier	Meister
			Conducteur de travaux	Polier
				Vorarbeiter
			Contremaître	Werkmeister
Freight Forwarder	Speditør	Expediteur	Commissionnaire de transport	Spediteur
General Manager (G.M.)	Generaldirektør	Algemeen directeur	Directeur	Generaldirektor
			Directeur général	Leitender Direktor
		Directeur-generaal	Gérant	
			Président-directeur général	
Head of (the ...) Section/ Division/ Department	Afdelingsleder	Hoofd sectie	Secrétaire d'administration (Public Admin.)	Abteilungsleiter
			Sous-directeur de ... (Public Admin.)	
Head of Customer Relations	Servicechef	Hoofd klanten- dienst	Directeur du service maintenance	Leiter der Kundendienst- abteilung
Head of Organizational Development [Organisational Planning]	Organisationschef	Hoofd organisatie- afdeling	Directeur de la planification administrative	Leiter/Direktor der Betriebs- organisation
				Leiter/Direktor der Organisations- abteilung
Head/Chief/Senior	Chef	Chef	Chef	Chef
	Direktør	Hoofd	Directeur	Direktor
	Leder			Leiter

ITALIAN	NORWEGIAN	PORTUGUESE	SPANISH	SWEDISH
Capo reparto	Arbeidsleder Bas Formann	Capataz Contramestre	Capataz Contramaestre	Arbetsledare
Spedizioniere	Speditør	Agente de expedição	Agente de Transportes Comisionista de Transporte	Speditör
Direttore generale	Administrerende direktør	Director-Geral	Director General	Direktör Verkställande direktör
Capo ufficio	Avdelingsdirektør Avdelingssjef	Chefe de repartição	Jefe de(l) Departamento	Avdelningschef
Capo servizio	Servicesjef	Chefe de serviços de assistência	Jefe del Servicio Post-ventas	Chef kundtjänst
Capo dei servizi organizzativi	Organisasjonssjef	Gestor de assuntos de organização	Jefe de la Planificación Administrativa	Organisationschef
Capo	Sjef	Chefe	Jefe	Chef

ENGLISH	DANISH	DUTCH	FRENCH	GERMAN
Inspector	Inspektør	Inspecteur	Inspecteur	Inspektor Prüfer
Instructor	Instruktør	Instructeur	Instructeur	Ausbilder
Internal Auditor	Intern revisor	Accountant Interne audit	Audit interne	Innenrevisor Wirtschafts- prüfer
Journalist	Journalist	Journalist	Journaliste	Journalist
Laboratory Manager	Laboratoriechef Laboratorieleder	Laboratoriumchef	Chef de laboratoire Directeur de laboratoire	Laborleiter
Lawyer/Attorney [Solicitor]	Advokat	Advocaat	Avocat	Rechtsanwalt
Lecturer [Reader]	Docent	Lector	Maître de conférences	Dozent Lektor
Legal Adviser (Bank)	Bankjurist	Rechtskundig bankadviseur	Conseil juridique (de la banque ...) Conseiller juridique (de la banque ...) Juriste bancaire	Bankjurist Bankjustitiar Banksyndikus
Legal Adviser (Company)	Aktieselskabs-jurist	Rechtskundig adviseur bij een bedrijf	Conseil(ler) juridique	Unternehmens-berater
Librarian	Bibliotekar	Bibliothecaris	Bibliothécaire	Bibliothekar
Logistics Manager	Logistikchef	Hoofd logistiek	Directeur de la logistique	Leiter/Direktor der Logistik-abteilung
M.D.	Læge	Dokter Geneesheer	Médecin	Arzt

ITALIAN	NORWEGIAN	PORTUGUESE	SPANISH	SWEDISH
Ispettore	Inspektør	Inspector	Inspector	Inspektör
Instruttore	Instruktør	Instrutor	Instructor	Instruktör
Revisore interno	Internrevisor	Auditor interno Revisor interno	Auditor Interno	Internrevisor
Giornalista	Journalist	Jornalista	Periodista	Journalist
Direttore del laboratorio	Laboratoriesjef	Chefe de laboratório	Jefe de Laboratorio	Laboratoriechef
Avvocato	Advokat	Advogado	Abogado	Advokat Jurist
Docente Docente universitário	Dosent	Docente universitário	(Professor) Agregado Catedrálico Universitario Agregado	Docent Universitets- lektor
Giurista bancario	Bankjurist	Assessor jurídico bancário	Asesor Jurídico de Bancos	Bankjurist
(Consulente) legale dell' azienda	Juridisk rådgiver	Assessor jurídico de empresa	Asesor Jurídico de la Sociedad	Bolagssjurist
Bibliotecario	Bibliotekar	Bibliotecário	Bibliotecario	Bibliotekarie
Capo dei servizi logistici	Logistikksjef	Chefe do departamento de logística	Jefe de Logística	Logistikchef
Medico	Lege	Médico	Médico	Läkare

ENGLISH	DANISH	DUTCH	FRENCH	GERMAN
Manager	Chef	Chef	Chef	Chef
		Hoofd	Directeur	Leiter
Marketing (and Sales) Manager	Salgschef	Marketing (en sales) manager	Directeur marketing (et ventes)	Verkaufsleiter Vertriebsleiter
Marketing Assistant	Marketing-assistent	Assistent marketing	Assistant marketing	Assistent der Marketingleitung
Marketing Director	Marketing-direktør	Directeur verkoop Hoofd verkoop Marketing directeur	Directeur marketing	Leiter der Marketingabtei-lung
Master Mechanic	Værkfører	Ploegbaas Voorman	Chef d'atelier Contremaître	Vorarbeiter Mechaniker-meister Werkmeister
Mayor	Borgmester	Burgemeester	Maire	Bürgermeister
Notary Public	Notarius publicus	Notaris	Notaire	Notar
Office Manager	Bureauchef Kontorchef	Kantoorchef	Chef de bureau	Büroleiter Geschäftstellen-leiter
Patent Engineer	Patentingeniør	Octrooitechnicus	Ingénieur de brevets	Patentingenieur
Permanent Secretary	Departements-chef Statssekretær	Staatssecretaris	Secrétaire d'Etat	Staatssekretär

ITALIAN	NORWEGIAN	PORTUGUESE	SPANISH	SWEDISH
Capo	Direktør	Chefe	Director	Chef
Responsabile	Sjef	Director	Gerente	Direktör
			Jefe	
Capo servizio vendite Direttore vendite Responsabile servizio marketing e vendite	Salgssjef	Chefe de marketing e vendas	Director/Jefe de Ventas	Försäljningschef
Assistente al marketing	Markedsassistent	Assistente de marketing	Asistente de Marketing	Marknadsassistent
Direttore servizio marketing	Markedsdirektør	Director do departamento de marketing	Director de Mercados	Marknadsdirektör
Capo mastro	Verksmester	Capataz Chefe de oficina Contramestre	Contramaestre	Verkmästare
Sindaco	Ordfører	Burgomestre	Alcalde	Borgmästare Kommunstyrelsens ordförande
Notario	Notarius publicus	Notário Público	Notario	Notarius publicus
Capo ufficio	Kontorsjef	Chefe de escritório	Jefe de Oficina	Kontorschef
Ingegnere Ufficio brevetti	Patentingeniør	Engenheiro de patentes	Ingeniero de Patentes	Patentingenjör
Segretario dello Stato	Departementstråd	Secretário de Estado	Secretario de Estado	Statssekreterare

ENGLISH	DANISH	DUTCH	FRENCH	GERMAN
Personnel Director/ Manager	Personaledirektør Personalechef	Directeur perso-neeldienst Personeelschef	Directeur du personnel Directeur du service du personnel Chef du personnel Chef du service du personnel	Personalchef Leiter/Direktor der Personalabteilung Personalchef Personalleiter
Pharmacist [Chemist]	Apoteker	Apotheker	Pharmacien	Apotheker
Physician	Læge	Arts Dokter Geneesheer	Médecin	Arzt
Planning Director	Planlægnings-direktør	Hoofd planningsafdeling	Directeur de la planification Directeur du service de planification	Leiter/Direktor der Planungsabtei-lung
Plant Manager	Fabrikschef Fabriksleder	Fabrieksdirecteur	Directeur d'usine	Fabrikdirektor Werksdirektor Werksleiter
President (CEO) [Group/ Managing Director]	Koncernchef	Voorzitter (van een concern)	Président du groupe Président-direc-teur général	Konzernchef
Principal [Headmaster/ Headmistress]	Rektor	Directeur Rector Schoolhoofd	Directeur	Direktor Oberstudien-direktor Rektor

ITALIAN	NORWEGIAN	PORTUGUESE	SPANISH	SWEDISH
Direttore del personale	Personaldirektør	Director do departamento de pessoal	Director de Personal	Personaldirektör
Capo del personale	Personalsjef	Chefe de pessoal	Jefe de Personal	Personalchef
Farmacista	Apoteker	Farmacêutico	Farmacéutico	Apotekare
Medico	Lege	Médico	Médico	Läkare
Direttore della pianificazione	Planleggings-direktør	Director de planeamento	Director de Planificación	Plannings-direktör
Capo fabbrica	Disponent	Chefe de fábrica	Directeur de (la) Fábrica	Disponent
	Fabrikksjef			Fabrikschef
	Teknisk direktør			Teknisk chef
	Teknisk sjef			Teknisk direktör
	Verkssjef			Verkschef
Presidente del Gruppo	Konsernsjef	Presidente de grupo empresarial	Presidente del Grupo	Koncernchef
				Verkställande direktör
Preside	Rektor	Director de estabelecimento de encino	Director	Rektor
Rettore			Rector	

ENGLISH	DANISH	DUTCH	FRENCH	GERMAN
Product Manager	Produktchef	Product manager	Chef de produit	Produktmanager
Production Director/ Manager	Produktions- direktør Produktionschef	Productiedirecteur Produktiechef Produktieleider	Directeur de la production Chef de fabrication	Fertigungsleiter Produktionsleder Betriebsleiter Produktionsleiter
Professor	Professor	Professor	Professeur	Professor
Programmer	Programmør	Programmeur	Programmeur	Programmierer
Project Leader/Manager	Projektleder	Projectleider	Chef de projet Responsable de projet	Projektleiter
Project Officer [Enterprise Officer—Local Government]	Erhvervsråds- sekretæer	Ambtenaar belast met contacten bedrijfsleven- overheid	Secrétaire à la promotion des enterprises	Referent für Unternehmens- beratung
Prosecutor	Anklager	Procureur	Procureur	Staatsanwalt
Public Relations (P.R./Informa- tion/Informa- tion Services) Director	Informations- direktør	Directeur informatiedienst Directeur PR- afdeling	Directeur des relations extérieures Directeur des relations publiques Directeur du service information	Leiter der Abteilung Öffentlichkeits- arbeit Leiter der PR- Abteilung Pressechef Pressesprecher
Purchaser	Indkøber	Inkoper	Acheteur	Einkäufer
Purchasing Manager	Indkøbschef	Inkoopchef	Directeur des achats	Einkaufsleiter Leiter der Einkaufsabteilung

ITALIAN	NORWEGIAN	PORTUGUESE	SPANISH	SWEDISH
Responsabile prodotti	Produktsjef	Gestor de produto	Jefe de Producto	Produktchef
Direttore della produzione Responsabile della produzione	Produksjonssjef Driftssjef Produksjonssjef	Director de produção Chefe de produção	Director de Producción Jefe de Producción	Produktions-direktör Driftschef Produktionschef
Professore	Professor	Professor	Profesor	Professor
Programmatore	Programmerer	Programador	Programador	Programmerare
Responsabile/ Capo del progetto	Prosjektleder	Supervisor de projecto	Consejero para la Promoción de Empresas	Projektledare
Segretario dell'Industria	Næringsutviklings-konsulent	Assessor de actividades comerciais e industriais	Jefe de Proyecto(s)	Näringslivs-sekreterare
Procuratore della Repubblica	Aktor Anklager Statsadvokat	Representante do Ministério Público	Fiscal Ministerio Fiscal Ministerio Público	Åklagare
Direttore servizio informazioni	Informasjons-direktør	Director de informação	Director de Información Director de Relaciones Públicas	Informations-direktör
Adetto agli acquisti	Innkjøper	Comprador	Comprador	Inköpare
Capo servizio acquisti	Innkjøpssjef	Chefe de compras	Jefe de Compras	Inköpschef

ENGLISH	DANISH	DUTCH	FRENCH	GERMAN
Quality Control Manager	Kvalitetschef	Hoofd kwaliteits-afdeling	Chef du service contrôle qualité	Leiter des Qualitätswesens
Real Estate Manager [Estate Manager]	Ejendoms-administrator Ejendomsleder	Directeur vast-goedadministratie	Chef/Directeur de la gestion immobilière	Leiter/Direktor der Grundstücks-verwaltung
Regional Director/ Manager	Regionschef	Regionale chef/directeur	Directeur régional	Bezirksleiter Gebietsleiter
Research Manager	Forskningschef Forskningsleder	Hoofd onder-zoeksafdeling	Directeur de la recherche	Leiter der Forschungs-abteilung
Safety Manager	Sikkerhedschef	Hoofd veiligheids-dienst	Chef du service de sécurité Directeur du service de sécurité	Werkschutzleiter
Sales Engineer	Salgsingeniør	Technisch verkoper	Ingénieur commercial	Verkaufs-ingenieur Vertriebs-ingenieur
Sales Manager	Salgschef Salgsleder	Verkoopchef	Chef de ventes Chef du service des ventes Directeur des ventes Directeur du ser-vice des ventes	Leiter/Direktor der Organisations-abteilung Verkaufsleiter Vertriebsleiter
Sales Representative	Repræsentant Sælger	Handelsvertregen-woordiger	Représentant Représentant de commerce Vendeur	Handelsvertreter Verkäufer
Salesman	Sælger	Verkoper	Vendeur	Verkäufer

ITALIAN	NORWEGIAN	PORTUGUESE	SPANISH	SWEDISH
Capo del servizio controllo qualitá	Kvalitetssjef	Chefe de controle de qualidade	Jefe del Servicio Control de Calidad	Kvalitetschef
Capo servizio gestione immobili	Eiendomssjef	Chefe do departamento de imóveis	Jefe de Gestión Inmobiliaria	Fastighetschef
Direttore regionale	Regionsjef	Director regional	Director Regional	Regionschef
Direttore del servizio ricerca	Forskningssjef	Chefe do departamento de investigação	Jefe de Investigación	Forskningschef
Responsabile Sicurezza	Sikkerhetssjef	Chefe de segurança	Jefe del Servicio de Seguridad	Säkerhetschef
Ingegnere tecnico-commerciale	Salgsingeniør	Engenheiro de vendas	Ingeniero Comercial	Försäljningsingenjör
Responsabile vendite	Salgsleder Salgssjef	Chefe de vendas	Jefe de Ventas Jefe del Servicio de Ventas	Försäljningschef Säljledare
Rappresentante	Representant Selger	Agente de vendas Representante	Agente Comercial	Försäljare Säljare
Venditore	Ekspeditør Selger	Vendedor	Vendedor	Försäljare Säljare

ENGLISH	DANISH	DUTCH	FRENCH	GERMAN
Secretary	Sekretær	Secretaris	Secrétaire	Schriftführer
		Sectiehoofd		Sekretär
Security Manager	Sikkerhedschef	Chef veiligheids-dienst	Chef du service de sécurité	Werkschutzleiter
			Directeur du service de sécurité	
Senior Executive Secretary	Direktions-sekretær	Directiesecretaris	Secrétaire de direction	Sekretär der Geschäftslei-tung
Service Engineer	Serviceingeniør	Ingenieur onder-houdsafdeling	Ingénieur de maintenance	Wartungs-ingenieur
			Technicien d'entretien	Wartungs-techniker
Service Manager	Servicechef	Hoofd klantendienst	Chef du service après-vente	Leiter der Kundendienst-abteilung
			Directeur du service maintenance	
Shipping (Department) Manager	Shippingschef	Hoofd expeditie-afdeling	Chef des expéditions	Leiter der Versandab-teilung
Shipping Agent	Speditør	Expediteur	Commissionaire de transport	Spediteur
Special Assistant to ... [Personal Assistant (P.A.) to Managing Director]	Direktions-sekretær	Directiesecretaris	Secrétaire de direction	Sekretär der Geschäftsleitung
Staff Director	Personaledirektør	Directeur perso-neeldienst	Directeur du personnel	Personalchef
			Directeur du service du personnel	

ITALIAN	NORWEGIAN	PORTUGUESE	SPANISH	SWEDISH
Segretario	Fullmektig Sekretær	Secretário	Secretario	Sekreterare
Responsabile Sicurezza	Sikkerhetssjef	Chefe de segurança	Jefe del Servicio de Seguridad	Säkerhetschef
Segretario Amministratore delegato	Sjefssekretær	Secretário do Director-Geral	Secretario de Dirección	VD-sekreterare
Ingegnere di manutenzione Tecnico di manutenzione	Serviceingeniør	Engenheiro de serviços de assistência	Ingeniero de Mantenimiento	Serviceingenjör
Capo servizio	Servicesjef	Chefe de serviços de assistência	Jefe de Mantenimiento Jefe del Servicio de Mantenimiento	Servicechef
Capo servizio spedizioni via mare	Transportsjef	Chefe de despachos por via marítima Chefe de embarque	Comisionista de Transporte Jefe de Embarques Jefe de Expedición	Skeppningschef
Spedizioniere	Speditør	Agente de expedição	Agente de Transportes	Speditör
Segretario dell'Amministra- tore delegato	Sjefssekretær	Secretário do Director-Geral	Secretario de Dirección Secretario de la Dirección General Secretario del Director Gerente	VD-sekreterare
Direttore del personale	Personaldirektør	Director do depar- tamento de pessoal	Director de Personal	Personal- direktör

111

ENGLISH	DANISH	DUTCH	FRENCH	GERMAN
Staff Manager	Personalechef	Personeelschef	Chef du personnel Chef du service du personnel	Leiter/Direktor der Personalabteilung Personalchef Personalleiter
Structural ...	Bygnings...	Bouw...	... du bâtiment	Bau...
Supervisor [Overseer]	Værkfører	Ploegbaas Voorman	Chef d'atelier Contremaître	Vorarbeiter Werkmeister
Surveyor	Inspektør	Inspecteur	Inspecteur	Inspektor
Systems Analyst	Systemansvarlig	Systeemanalist	Analyste (de) systèmes	Systemanalytiker
Systems Engineer	Systemansvarlig	Systeemanalist	Analyste (de) systèmes	Systemanalytiker System-programmierer
Systems Manager	Systemschef	Hoofd systeem-afdeling	Responsable système(s)	Leiter der EDV-Abteilung
Technical Director	Teknisk direktør	Directeur technische dienst Technisch directeur	Chef du service technique Directeur du service technique Directeur technique	Technischer Leiter/Direktor
Trainee	Praktikant	Stagiair	Stagiaire	Praktikant

ITALIAN	NORWEGIAN	PORTUGUESE	SPANISH	SWEDISH
Capo del personale	Personalsjef	Chefe de pessoal	Jefe de Personal	Personalchef
... edile	Bygge...	... de contrução	... de Construcciones	Byggnads...
	Bygnings...		... de Obras	
Responsabile dello stabilimento	Verksmester	Capataz Chefe de oficina Contramestre	Contramaestre	Arbetsledare Verkmästare
Inspettore	Inspektør	Inspector	Inspector	Inspektör
Analista di sistemi	Systemansvarlig	Analista de sistemas	Analista de Sistemas	Systemerare
Ingegnere sistemista	Systemerer	Analista de sistemas	Analista de Sistemas	Systemerare
Capo servizio analisi di sistemi	IT-sjef Systemsjef	Chefe de análise de sistemas	Jefe de Sistemas	Systemchef
Direttore tecnico	Teknisk direktør Teknisk sjef	Director de servicios técnicos	Director Técnico	Teknisk chef Teknisk direktör
Apprendista	Praktikant	Estagiário	Aspirante en Prácticas Estudiante en Prácticas	Praktikant

ENGLISH	DANISH	DUTCH	FRENCH	GERMAN
Transport Manager	Transportchef	Hoofd transport-afdeling	Chef du service des transports Directeur du service des transports	Leiter/Direktor der Frachtabteilung Leiter/Direktor der Transportab-teilung Leiter/Direktor der Versandabteilung
Veterinarian [Veterinary Officer/Surgeon]	Dyrlæge	Dierenarts	Vétérinaire	Tierarzt
Vice President [Deputy Managing Director]	Vice-general-direktør	Adjunct-alge-meendirecteur	Directeur général adjoint	Stellvertretender Generaldirektor
Vice-Chancellor	Rektor	Rector	Recteur	Rektor
Warehouse Supervisor [Stores Manager]	Lagerchef	Magazijnbeheerder	Chef-magasinier	Lagerverwalter

ITALIAN	NORWEGIAN	PORTUGUESE	SPANISH	SWEDISH
Responsabile transporti	Transportsjef	Chefe do departamento de transportes	Jefe de Transportes	Transportchef
Veterenario	Veterinær	Veterinário	Veterinario	Veterinär
Viceamministratore delegato	Viseadministrerende direktør	Vice-gerente	Subdirector Vicegerente	Vice verkställande direktör
Preside Rettore	Rektor	Reitor	Rector	Rektor
Responsabile magazzini	Lagersjef	Chefe de armazém	Jefe de Almacén	Lagerchef

CROSS REFERENCE TITLES INDEX

International business titles, as they appear in any of the ten most important European languages, are listed alphabetically below in **bold italics** with their language identification abbreviation in parenthesis and their American title equivalent in Roman type. For example, the title **Botschafter** is described below as (DE) for German and defined as Ambassador.

Non-English letters—ø, o, ü, å, ä for example—are alphabetized in this index as if they had no diacritical markings, except where they are the *initial* letter of a word. In those cases, the capital letter appears at the *end* of the listings for the standard letter. If an elipsis is used at the beginning of a title—as in "... Adjoint"—the title is found at the end of the listing for that letter.

As language borders do not coincide with national frontiers, we have used special abbreviations to designate the ten languages found in this Index. They are as follows: British (GB), Danish (DK), Dutch (NL), French (FR), German (DE), Italian (IT), Norwegian (NO),Portuguese (PT), Spanish (ES), and Swedish (SE).

A

Abogado (ES) Lawyer/Attorney

Abteilungsleiter (DE) Departmental Director/Manager/Director of (the...) Department ... /Head of (the...) Section/Department/Division

Accountant (NL) Auditor/Internal Auditor

Acheteur (FR) Buyer/Purchaser

Actuaire (FR) Actuary

Actuario (ES) Actuary

Actuário (PT) Actuary

Actuaris (NL) Actuary

ADB-chef (SE) Computer/Data Processing Manager

Addetto agli acquisti (IT) Purchaser

Adjoint (FR) Assistant

Adjunct- ... (NL) Assistant .../Deputy...

Adjunct-algemeendirecteur (NL) Vice President; Deputy General Manager; Deputy Managing Director

Adjunct-directeur (NL) Assistant Director

Administrador de Finanzas (ES) Chief Financial Officer; Financial Manager

Administrasjons-direktør (NO) Director of Administration

Administrasjonsdirektør (NO) Director of Administration

Administrasjonssjef (NO) Director/Manager of Administration

Administrateur financier (FR) Chief Financial Officer/Financial Manager

Administratief directeur (NL) Director of Administration

Administrativ direktör (SE) Director of Administration

Administrative Director (GB) Director of Administration

Administrative Manager (GB) Director of Administration

Administrerende direktør (DK NO) Managing Director

Advisieur (NL) Consultant

Advocaat (NL) Lawyer/Attorney

Advogado (PT) Lawyer/Attorney

Advokat (DK NO SE) Lawyer/Attorney

Afdelingschef (DK) Departmental Manager

Afdelingsdirecteur (NL) Departmental/Deputy Director/Director of (the ...) Department ...

Afdelingsdirektør (DK) Director of (the ...) Department ...

Afdelingshoofd (NL) Departmental Manager

Afdelingsleder (DK) Head of (the ...) Section/Department/Division

Agent (DK NL FR DE NO SE) Agent

Agent de maîtrise (FR) Foreman
Agente de Transportes (ES) Shipping Agent
Agente de vendas (PT) Sales Representative
Agente (IT PT ES) Agent
Agente (IT) Broker
Agente Comercial (ES) Commercial/Sales
  Representative
Agente de compras (PT) Buyer
Agente de expedição (PT) Freight Forwarder/
  Shipping Agent
Agente de Seguros (ES) Broker
Agente de Transportes (ES) Freight Forwarder
Agente de vendas (PT) Commercial Representative
Agente intermediário (PT) Broker
Aktieselskabsjurist (DK) Legal Adviser
  (Company)
Aktor (NO) Prosecutor
Aktuar (DK DE NO) Actuary
Aktuarie (SE) Actuary
Alcalde (ES) Mayor
Algemeen directeur (NL) Director-General/General
  Manager/Managing Director
Ambasciatore (IT) Ambassador
Ambassadeur (NL FR) Ambassador
Ambassadør (DK NO) Ambassador
Ambassadör (SE) Ambassador
Ambtenaar belast met contacten
  bedrijfslevenoverheid (NL) Project Officer
Amministratore delegato (IT) Managing
  Director (M.D.)
Analista de Sistemas (ES) Systems Analyst/
  Engineer
Analista de sistemas (PT) Systems Analyst/
  Engineer
Analista di sistemi (IT) Systems Analyst
Analyste (de) systèmes (FR) Systems Analyst/
  Engineer
Anklager (DK NO) Prosecutor
Apoderado (ES) Executive Assistant
Apotekare (SE) Pharmacist
Apoteker (DK NO) Pharmacist
Apotheker (DE NL) Pharmacist
Apprendista (IT) Trainee
Arbeidsleder (NO) Foreman
Arbejdsleder (DK) Foreman
Arbetsledare (SE) Foreman
Architect (NL) Architect
Architecte (FR) Architect
Architekt (DE) Architect
Architetto (IT) Architect
Arkitekt (DK NO SE) Architect
Arquitecto (PT ES) Architect
Arts (NL) Physician
Arzt (DE) Physician

Asesor Jurídico de Bancos (ES) Legal Adviser
  (Bank)
Asesor Jurídico de la Sociedad (ES) Legal Adviser
  (Company)
Asistente (ES) Assistant
Asistente de Marketing (ES) Assistant Marketing
  Manager/Marketing Assistant
Aspirante en Prácticas (ES) Trainee
Assessor de actividades comerciais e industriais
  (PT) Project Officer
Assessor jurídico bancário (PT) Legal Adviser
  (Bank)
Assessor jurídico de empresa (PT) Legal Adviser
  (Company)
Assistant (FR) Assistant
Assistant de marketing (FR) Assistant/Deputy
  Marketing Manager/Marketing Assistant
Assistent marketing (NL) Marketing Assistant
Assistent (DK NL DE NO SE) Assistant
Assistent der Marketingleitung (DE) Assistant
  Marketing Manager
Assistent der Marketingleitung (DE) Marketing
  Assistant/Deputy Marketing Manager
Assistent marketing (NL) Assistant/Deputy
  Marketing Manager
Assistente (IT PT) Assistant
Assistente al marketing (IT) Assistant/Deputy
  Marketing Manager/Marketing Assistant
Assistente de Marketing (ES) Assistant Marketing
  Manager
Assistente de marketing (PT) Assistant/Deputy
  Marketing Manager/Marketing Assistant
Assisterende direktør (NO) Assistant Director
Assisterende... (NO) Assistant .../Deputy...
Attuario (IT) Actuary
Audit (FR) Auditor
Audit interne (FR) Internal Auditor
Auditor (PT ES) Auditor
Auditor Interno (PT ES) Internal Auditor
Aufsichtsratsvorsitzender (DE) Chairman of the
  Board (of Directors)
Ausbilder (DE) Instructor
Auxiliar (ES) Assistant
Avdelningschef (SE) Head/Director of (the ...)
  Section/Department/Division
Avdelningssjef (NO) Head/Manager of (the ...)
  Section/Division/Department
Avdelningdirektør (NO) Departmental Director
Avdelningsdirektör (SE) Departmental Director
Avocat (FR) Lawyer/Attorney
Avvocato (IT) Lawyer/Attorney
Ayudante del ... (ES) Assistant
Åklagare (SE) Prosecutor
... adjoint (FR) Deputy ...

... *Adjunto* (ES) Deputy ...
... *Adjunct*—(NL) Assistant .../Deputy ...
... *adjunto* (PT) Deputy ...
... *aggiunto* (IT) Deputy ...
... *assistent* (DE) Deputy ...
... *assisterende* ... (NO) Deputy ...
... *assistente* (PT) Deputy ...
... *auxiliar* (PT) Deputy ...

B

Bank Legal Adviser (GB) Legal Adviser (Bank)
Bankdirecteur (NL) Bank Director/Manager
Bankdirektor (DE) Bank Director/Manager
Bankdirektør (DK NO) Bank Director/Manager
Bankdirektör (SE) Bank Director/Manager
Bankjurist (DE) Legal Adviser (Bank)
Bankjustitiar (DE) Legal Adviser (Bank)
Banksjef (NO) Bank Manager
Banksyndikus (DE) Legal Adviser (Bank)
Bas (NO) Foreman
Bau... (DE) Structural ...
Bau... (DE) Building ...
Bauleiter (Bauindustrie) (DE) Foreman
Berater (DE) Consultant
Bestyrelsesformand (DK) Chairman of the Board
  (of Directors)
Betriebsleiter (DE) Production Director/Manager
Bezirksleiter (DE) Regional/District Director/
  Manager
Bibliotecario (IT ES) Librarian
Bibliotecário (PT) Librarian
Bibliotekar (DK NO) Librarian
Bibliotekarie (SE) Librarian
Bibliothecaris (NL) Librarian
Bibliothécaire (FR) Librarian
Bibliothekar (DE) Librarian
Biträdande ... (SE) Assistant .../Deputy ...
Boekhouder (NL) Accountant
Bogholder (DK) Accountant
Bolagsjurist (SE) Legal Adviser (Company)
Borgmästare (SE) Mayor
Borgmester (DK) Mayor
Botschafter (DE) Ambassador
Bouw...(NL) Building .../Structural ...
Brandchef (SE) Fire Marshal
Brandschutzleiter (DE) Fire Marshal
Brandsikkerhedschef (DK) Fire Marshal
Brannsjef (NO) Fire Marshal
Buchhalter (DE) Accountant
Bureauchef (DK) Office Manager
Burgemeester (NL) Mayor
Bürgermeister (DE) Mayor
Burgomestre (PT) Mayor

Büroleiter (DE) Office Manager
Bygge... (NO) Building .../Structural ...
Byggnads... (SE) Structural .../Building ...
Bygnings... (DK NO) Building .../Structural ...
Byråsjef (NO) Deputy Chief of Mission

C

Canceler (PT) Deputy Chief of Mission
Cancelliere capo (IT) Deputy Chief of Mission
Canciller (ES) Deputy Chief of Mission
Capataz (ES PT) Foreman
Capataz (PT) Master Mechanic/Supervisor
Capo (IT) Chief/Head/Manager/Senior
Capo contabile (IT) Chief Accountant
Capo dei servizi organizzativi (IT) Head of
  Organizational Development
Capo dei servizi informatici (IT) Computer/Data
  Processing Manager
Capo dei servizi logistici (IT) Logistics Manager
Capo del personale (IT) Staff Manager/Head of
  Staff Section/Department/Division
Capo del servizio controllo qualitá (IT) Quality
  Control Manager
Capo del servizio finanziario (IT) Chief Financial
  Officer
Capo dell'ufficio di progettazione (IT) Drafting
  Office Manager
Capo distretto (IT) District Manager
Capo distribuzione (IT) Distribution Manager
Capo divisione (IT) Divisional Manager
Capo fabbrica (IT) Factory/Plant Manager
Capo mastro (IT) Master Mechanic
Capo reparto (IT) Departmental Manager/
  Foreman
Capo servizi amministrativi (IT) Director/
  Manager of Administration
Capo servizio (IT) Service Manager/Head of
  Customer Service Section/Department/Division
Capo servizio acquisti (IT) Chief/Head Buyer/
  Purchaser
Capo servizio gestione immobili (IT) Real Estate
  Manager
Capo servizio spedizioni via mare (IT) Shipping
  (Department) Manager
Capo servizio vendite (IT) Marketing (and Sales)
  Manager
Capo sezione (IT) Departmental Manager
Capo ufficio (IT) Head of (the...) Section/Division
  Department
Capo ufficio (IT) Office Manager
Capo ufficio vendite esportazione (IT) Export
  Manager
Carrier (GB) Freight Forwarder

Catedrálico Universitario Agregado (ES) Lecturer
Chanceler (PT) Deputy Chief of Mission
Chef (DK NL FR DE SE) Head/Chief/Senior/
  Manager
Chef comptable (FR) Chief/Senior/Head
  Accountant
Chef d'atelier (FR) Foreman; Master Mechanic;
  Supervisor
Chef de laboratoire (FR) Laboratory Manager
Chef de bureau (FR) Office Manager
Chef de chancellerie (FR) Deputy Chief of Mission
Chef de département (FR) Divisional Director/
  Manager
Chef de division (FR) Divisional Director/Manager
Chef de la distribution (FR) Distribution Manager
Chef de la formation (FR) Chief Training Officer
Chef de la gestion immobiliére (FR) Real Estate
  Manager
Chef de produit (FR) Product Manager
Chef de projet (FR) Project Leader/Manager
Chef de service (FR) Departmental Director/
  Manager
Chef des expéditions (FR) Shipping (Department)
  Manager
Chef des exportations (FR) Export Manager
Chef des services de lutte contre l'incendie (FR) Fire
  Marshal
Chef des ventes (FR) Distribution/Sales Manager
Chef du bureau d'études (FR) Drafting Office
  Manager
Chef du personnel (FR) Staff Manager/Head of
  Personnel Section/Department/Division
Chef du service après-vente (FR) Service Manager
Chef du service contrôle qualité (FR) Quality
  Control Manager
Chef du service de sécurité (FR) Safety Manager
Chef du service de sécurité (FR) Security Manager
Chef du service (des) exportations (FR) Head of
  Export Section/Department/Divison
Chef du service des transports (FR) Transportation
  Section/Department/Division Manager
Chef du service des ventes (FR) Sales Manager
Chef du service contrats (FR) Contracts Manager
Chef du service de sécurité (FR) Head of Security/
  Safety Section/Department/Division
Chef du service des ventes (FR) Distribution
  Manager
Chef du service développement (FR) Development
  Manager
Chef du service du personnel (FR) Head of
  Personnel
Chef du service du personnel (FR) Staff Manager

Chef du service financier (FR) Chief Financial
  Officer; Financial Manager; Head of Financial
  Section/Department
Chef du service formation (FR) Chief Training
  Officer
Chef kundtjänst (SE) Head of Customer Relations
Chef du service local de police (FR) Chief of Police
Chef du service(des) exportations (FR) Export
  Manager
Chef du service technique (FR) Technical Director
Chef- magasinier (FR) Warehouse Supervisor
Chef veiligheidsdienst (NL) Security Manager
Chefe (PT) Chief...
Chefe (PT) Head/Chief/Senior
Chefe (PT) Manager
Chefe administrativo (PT) Director/Manager of
  Administration
Chefe de alfândega (PT) Customs Director
Chefe de análise de sistemas (PT) Systems Manager
Chefe de armazém (PT) Warehouse Supervisor
Chefe de compras (PT) Purchasing Manager; Chief/
  Head Buyer/Purchaser
Chefe de construção (PT) Drafting Office Manager
Chefe de contabilidade (PT) Chief/Senior/Head
  Accountant
Chefe de controle de qualidade (PT) Quality
  Control Manager
Chefe de despachos por via marítima (PT)
  Shipping (Department) Manager
Chefe de distribução (PT) Distribution Manager
Chefe de divisão (PT) Divisional Director/Head/
  Manager
Chefe de embarque (PT) Shipping (Department)
  Manager
Chefe de escritório (PT) Office Manager
Chefe de exportações (PT) Export Manager
Chefe de fábrica (PT) Factory/Plant Manager
Chefe de laboratório (PT) Laboratory Manager
Chefe de marketing e vendas (PT) Marketing (and
  Sales) Manager
Chefe de oficina (PT) Master Mechanic; Overseer
Chefe de pessoal (PT) Staff Manager/Head of Staff
  Section/Department/Division
Chefe de publicidade (PT) Advertising Manager/
  Director
Chefe de secção (PT) Departmental Manager
Chefe de segurança (PT) Safety/Security Manager;
  Head of Safety/Security
  Section/Department/Division
Chefe de serviços de assistência (PT) Service
  Manager/Head of Customer Service Section/
  Department/Division

Chefe de serviço de luta contra os incêndios (PT) Fire Marshal

Chefe de sucursal (PT) Branch Manager

Chefe de vendas (PT) Sales Manager

Chefe do departamento de contratos (PT) Contracts Manager

Chefe do departamento de desenvolvimento (PT) Development Manager

Chefe do departamento de formação interna (PT) Senior/Chief Training Officer

Chefe do departamento de imóveis (PT) Real Estate Manager

Chefe do departamento de logística (PT) Logistics Manager

Chefe do departamento de pessoal (PT) Chief of Staff

Chefe dos serviços de informática (PT) Computer/Data Processing Manager

Chefe do departamento de investigação (PT) Research Manager

Chefe do departamento de transportes (PT) Transport Manager

Chefe regional (PT) District Manager

Chefe-Geral da Polícia (PT) Chief Constable

Chefingenieur (DE) Chief Engineer

Chefkonstrukteur (DE) Drafting Office Manager

Chefredakteur (DE) Editor-in-Chief

Chefredaktør (DK) Editor-in-Chief

Chefredaktör (SE) Editor-in-Chief

Chemist (GB) Pharmacist

Chief Constable (GB) Chief of Police

Chief Fire Officer (GB) Fire Marshal

Chirurgien-dentiste (FR) Dental Surgeon/Dentist

Comandante dei vigili del Fuoco (IT) Fire Marshal

Comisionista de Transporte (ES) Freight Forwarder/Shipping (Department) Manager

Commissaris van politie (NL) Chief of Police

Commissionnaire de transport (FR) Shipping Agent/Freight Forwarder

Company Legal Adviser (GB) Legal Adviser (Company)

Comprador (ES PT) Buyer/Purchaser

Compratore (IT) Buyer

Compatable (FR) Accountant

Concepteur-projecteur en chef (FR) Drafting Office Manager

Concepteur-rédacteur (FR) Copywriter

Conducteur de travaux (FR) Foreman

Conseil (FR) Consultant

Conseil juridique (de la banque...) (FR) Legal Adviser (Bank)

Conseil(ler) juridique (FR) Legal Adviser (Company)

Conseiller juridique (de la banque...) (FR) Legal Adviser (Bank)

*Conseiller (FR) Con*sultant

Consejero para la Promoción de Empresas (ES) Project Officer/Leader/Mager

Construtor (PT) Design Engineer

Cónsul (ES) Consul

Consul (FR NL) Consul

Cônsul (PT) Consul

Consulente (IT) Consultant

(Consulente) legale dell'azienda (IT) Legal Adviser (Company)

Consultant (FR) Consultant

Consultor (ES PT) Consultant

Contabile (IT) Accountant

Contabilista (PT) Accountant

Contador (ES) Accountant

Contramaestre (ES PT) Foreman; Master Mechanic; Supervisor

Contremaître (FR) Foreman; Master Mechanic; Supervisor

*Copy (IT) C*opywriter

Copy-Writer (PT) Copywriter

Copywriter (DK NL SE) Copywriter

Corredor (ES) Broker

Corretor (PT) Broker

Courtier (FR) Broker

Creativo (IT) Copywriter

D

Datachef (DK SE) Data Processing/Computer Manager

Datasjef (NO) Data Processing/Computer Manager

Delegado (ES) Agent

Dentista (IT ES) Dental Surgeon; Dentist

Departementschef (DK) Director of Administration/Permanent Secretary

Departementstråd (NO) Permanent Secretary

Deputy Managing Director (GB) Vice President

Diensthoofd brandbesrijding (NL) Fire Marshal

Dierenarts (NL) Veterinarian

Director de (I) Departamento (ES) Deputy Director

Directeur (FR) General Manager; Head/Chief/Senior/Manager; Director

Directeur (NL) Director; Principal

Directeur administratif (FR) Director of Administration

Directeur commercial (FR) Director of Sales (Marketing); Distribution Director

Directeur d'hôpital (FR) Hospital Director/Manager

Directeur d'usine (FR) Plant Manager

Directeur de banque (FR) Bank Director/Manager
Directeur de l'informatique (FR) Data Processing/ Computer Manager
Directeur de la distribution (FR) Distribution Manager
Directeur de la gestion immobiliére (FR) Real Estate Manager
Directeur de la logistique (FR) Logistics Manager
Directeur de la planification (FR) Director of Planning
Directeur de la planification administrative (FR) Head of Organizational Development
Directeur de la publicité (FR) Advertising Manager/Director
Directeur de la recherche (FR) Director/Manager of Research
Directeur de laboratoire (FR) Laboratory Manager
Directeur de service (FR) Departmental Director
Directeur de succursale (FR) Branch Manager
Directeur des achats (FR) Purchasing Manager; Chief/Head Buyer
Directeur des douanes (FR) Director of Customs
Directeur des exportations (FR) Export Director/ Manager; Director of the Export Section/ Department/Division
Directeur des hôpitaux (FR) Director of Medical (Hospital) Services
Directeur des relations extérieures (FR) Director of Public Relations
Directeur des ventes (FR) Sales Manager
Directeur des relations publiques (FR) Director of Public Relations
Directeur des ventes (FR) Director of Sales (Marketing) Section/Department/Division; Distribution Director/Manager
Directeur du bureau d'études (FR) Drafting Office Manager
Directeur du développement (FR) Development Manager
Directeur du marketing (FR) Director of Marketing
Directeur du personnel (FR) Personnel/Staff Director
Directeur du service (des) exportations (FR) Export Section/Department/Division Director
Directeur du service des transports (FR) Transportation Manager
Directeur du service des ventes (FR) Sales Manager
Directeur du service des ventes (FR) Director of Sales (Marketing); Distribution Director/ Manager
Directeur du service du personnel (FR) Personnel/ Staff Director; Chief Personnel/Staff Officer
Directeur du service financier (FR) Financial Manager/Head of Financial Services

Directeur du service formation (FR) Chief Training Officer
Directeur du service information (FR) Director of Public Relations
Directeur du service informatique (FR) Computer/ Data Processing Manager
Directeur du service maintenance (FR) Head of Customer Service; Service Manager
Directeur du service publicité (FR) Advertising Manager/Director
Directeur du service technique (FR) Technical Director
Directeur exportafdeling (NL) Director of Export Section/Department/Division
Directeur financiële afdeling (NL) Director of Finance
Directeur financier (FR) Chief Financial Officer/ Director; Financial Manager
Directeur général (FR) Director-General/General Manager
Directeur général adjoint (FR) Vice President; Deputy General Manager/Managing Director
Directeur informatiedienst (NL) Director of Public Relations
Directeur marketing (et ventes) (FR) Marketing (and Sales) Manager
Directeur marketing (FR) Marketing Director
Directeur onderzoeksafdeling (NL) Director of Research
Directeur personeelsdienst (NL) Personnel/Staff Director
Directeur PR-afdeling (NL) Director of Public Relations
Directeur régional (FR) Regional Director/ Manager
Directeur technique (FR) Technical Director
Directeur technische dienst (NL) Technical Director
Directeur vastgoedadministratie (NL) Real Estate Manager
Directeur verkoop (NL) Marketing Director
Directeur (École) (FR) Principal
Directeur-generaal (NL) Director-General; General Manager; Managing Director
Directiesecretaris (NL) Personal Assistant; Senior Executive Secretary
Director (de ...) (ES) Assistant Director
Director (ES) Principal
Director (NO) General Manager
Director (PT ES) Director/Manager
Director Adjunto de Comercialización (ES) Deputy Marketing Manager
Director Administrativo (ES) Director of Administration

Director administrativo (PT) Director of Administration
Director de Aduana (ES) Director of Customs
Director de alfândega (PT) Director of Customs
Director de Centro Hospitalario (ES) Director/ Manager of Medical (Hospital) Services
Director de departamento financeiro (PT) Chief/ Financial Officer; Director of Finance
Director de División (ES) Divisional Director
Director de estabelecimento de ensino (PT) Principal
Director de exportações (PT) Director of Export Section/Department/Division; Export Director
Director de Exportación (ES) Director of Export Section/Department/Division
Director de (la) Fábrica (ES) Plant Manager
Director de Hospitales (ES) Director/Manager of Medical (Hospital) Services
Director de hospital (PT) Director of Medical (Hospital) Services
Director de informação (PT) Director of Public Relations
Director de Investigación (ES) Director of Research
Director de Marketing (ES) Director of Marketing
Director de Mercados (ES) Marketing Director
Director de Personal (ES) Staff/Personnel Director
Director de planeamento (PT) Director of Planning Section/Department/Division
Director de Planificación (ES) Director/Head of Planning Section/Department/Division
Director de produção (PT) Production Director
Director de Producción (ES) Production Director
Director de Publicidad (ES) Advertising Manager/ Director
Director de Relaciones Públicas (ES) Director of Public Relations
Director de serviços técnicos (PT) Technical Director
Director de Sucursal (ES) Branch Manager
Director de Ventas (ES) Director of Sales (Marketing); Distribution Director
Director de(l) Departamento (ES) Assistant Director
Director de (la) Fábrica (ES) Factory Manager
Director del Banco (ES) Bank Director/ Manager
Director del Servicio Exportaciones (ES) Export Director
Director do departamento de investigação (PT) Director of Research
Director do departamento de marketing (PT) Director of Marketing
Director do departamento de pessoal (PT) Personnel Director; Staff Director

Director do departamento de vendas (PT) Director of Sales (Marketing) Section/Department/ Division; Distribution Director
Director Financiero (ES) Financial Director
Director General (ES) Director-General; General Manager; Managing Director
Director Regional (ES) District Manager
Director-Geral (PT) Director-General; General Manager; Managing Director
Director/Jefe de Ventas (ES) Marketing (and Sales) Manager
Director Regional (ES) Regional Director/Manager
Director regional (PT) Regional Director/Manager
Director Técnico (ES) Technical Director
Direktionssekretær (DK) Personal Assistant; Senior Executive Secretary
Direktor (DE) Director; Head/Chief/Senior; Principal
Direktør (DK) Director; Head/Chief/Senior
Direktør (NO) Manager; Director; Head/Chief/ Senior
Direktör (SE) Director/General Manager/Manager
Direktörassistent (SE) Assistant/Deputy Director
Direktor der Abteilung für Öffentlichkeitsarbeit (DE) Director
Direktor der Exportabteilung (DE) Export Director
Direktor der Finanzabteilung (DE) Financial Director
Direttore (IT) Director
Direttore aggiunto (IT) Assistant Director
Direttore amministrativo (IT) Director of Administration
Direttore d'ospedale (IT) Hospital Director/ Manager
Direttore del laboratorio (IT) Laboratory Manager
Direttore del marketing (IT) Director of Marketing
Direttore del personale (IT) Personnel/Staff Director
Direttore del reparto (IT) Departmental Director
Direttore del servizio ricerca (IT) Research Manager
Direttore della distribuzione (IT) Distribution Director
Direttore della dogana (IT) Director of Customs
Direttore della pianificazione (IT) Director of Planning
Direttore della produzione (IT) Production Director
Direttore regionale (IT) Regional Director/ Manager
Direttore della ricerca (IT) Director of Research
Direttore di banca (IT) Bank Director/Manager
Direttore di divisione (IT) Divisional Director
Direttore di filiale (IT) Branch Manager

Direttore finanziario (IT) Director of Finance
Direttore generale (IT) Director-General; General
Manager
Direttore servizi pubblicità (IT) Advertising
Manager/Director
Direttore servizio (marketing e) vendite (IT)
Director of Sales (and) Marketing
Direttore servizio esportazione (IT) Director of
Export Section/Department/Division
Direttore servizio informazioni (IT) Director of
Public Relations
Direttore servizio marketing (IT) Marketing
Director
Direttore servizio vendite (IT) Director of Sales
Direttore tecnico (IT) Technical Director
Direttore vendite (IT) Marketing (and Sales)
Manager
Direttore vendite esportazione (IT) Export Director
Disponent (SE) Factory Manager
Disponent (NO SE) Plant Manager
Distribusjonssjef (NO) Distribution Manager
Distributiedirecteur (NL) Distribution Director
Distributionschef (DK SE) Distribution Manager
Districtshoofd (NL) District Manager
Distriktschef (DK SE) District Manager
Distriktssjef (NO) District Manager
Directeur régional (FR) District Manager
Divisiedirecteur (NL) Divisional Director
Divisionschef (DK SE) Divisional Manager
Divisionschef (SE) Divisional Director
Divisionschefldirektør (DK) Divisional Director
Divisionsdirektor (DE) Divisional Director
Divisjonssjef (NO) Divisional Director/Manager
Docent (DK SE) Lecturer
Docente (IT) Lecturer
Docente universitário (IT PT) Lecturer
Dokter (NL) Physician
Dosent (NO) Lecturer
Dozent (DE) Lecturer
Drawing Office Manager (GB) Drafting Office
Manager
Driftssjef (NO) Production Director/Manager
Driftschef (SE) Production Director/Manager
Dyrlæge (DK) Veterinarian
... de Construcciones (ES) Structural ...
... de contrução (PT) Structural ...
... de Obras (ES) Structural ...
... de construção (PT) Building ...
... de Construcciones (ES) Building ...
... de Obras (ES) Building ...
... délégué (FR) Deputy ...
... du bâtiment (FR) Building .../Structural ...

E

EDB-chef (DK) Computer/Data Processing
Manager
EDB-sjef (NO) Computer/Data Processing
Manager
Eiendomssjef (NO) Real Estate Manager
Einkäufer (DE) Buyer/Purchaser
Einkaufsleiter (DE) Purchasing Manager/Chief/
Head
Ejendomsadministrator (DK) Real Estate Manager
Ejendomsleder (DK) Real Estate Manager
Ekonomdirektör (SE) Director of Finance
Ekonomichef (SE) Chief Accountant; Financial
Manager/Officer
Ekonomidirektör (SE) Chief Financial Director/
Officer
Ekspeditør (NO) Salesman
Eksportdirektør/sjef (NO) Director of Exports
Eksportchef (DK) Export Manager
Eksportdirektør (DK) Director of Export Section/
Department/Division
Eksportsjef (NO) Export Manager
Embaixador (PT) Ambassador
Embajador (ES) Ambassador
Encargado de la Formación del Personal (ES)
Chief Training Officer
Engenheiro (PT) ...Engineer
Engenheiro de desenvolvimento (PT) Development
Engineer
Engenheiro de patentes (PT) Patent Engineer
Engenheiro de vendas (PT) Sales Engineer
Engenheiro-chefe (PT) Chief Engineer
Entwicklungsingenieur (DE) Development
Engineer
Erhversrådssekretær (DK) Project Officer
Engenheiro de vendas (PT) Sales Engineer
Enterprise Officer **(Local Government)** (GB)
Project Officer
Erhversrådssekretær (DK) Project Officer
Expediteur (NL) Freight Forwarder
Exportchef (SE) Export Manager
Exportdirektør (DK NO) Export Director
Exportdirektör (SE) Director of Export Section/
Department/Division
Exportdirektör (SE) Export Director
... edile (IT) Building .../Structural ...

F

Fabrieksdirecteur (NL) Factory/Plant Manager
Fabrikdirektor (DE) Factory/Plant Manager
Fabrikksjef (NO) Factory/Plant Manager
Fabrikschef (DK SE) Factory/Plant Manager
Fabriksleder (DK) Factory/Plant Manager

Farmacéutico (ES) Pharmacist
Farmacêutico (PT) Pharmacist
Farmacista (IT) Pharmacist
Fastighetschef (SE) Real Estate Manager
Fertigungsleiter (DE) Production Director
Filiaalhouder (NL) Branch Manager
Filialchef (DK SE) Branch Manager
Filialleder (DK) Branch Manager
Filialleiter/direktor (DE) Branch Manager
Filialsjef (NO) Branch Manager
Finanschef (DK SE) Financial Manager
Finanssjef (NO) Financial Manager
Fiscal (ES) Prosecutor
Fondé de pouvoir (FR) Executive Assistant
Formand (DK) Chairman/person
Formann (NO) Foreman
Försäljare (SE) Sales Representative/Salesman
Försäljningschef (SE) Marketing (and Sales)
   Manager; Distribution Manager
Försäljningsingenjör (SE) Sales Engineer
Försäljningsdirektör (SE) Director of Sales
   (Marketing); Distribution Director
Forskningschef (DK SE) Research Manager
Foskningsleder (DK) Research Manager
Forskningssjef (NO) Research Manager
Forskningschef (DK SE) Director of Research
Forskningsleder (DK) Director of Research
Forskningssjef (NO) Director of Research
Förvaltningschef (SE) Director/Manager of
   Administration
Forvaltningschef (DK) Director/Manager of
   Administration
Forvaltningssjef (NO) Director/Manager of
   Administration

G

Gebietsleiter (DE) Regional Director/Manager
Geneesheer (NL) Physician
Generaldirektor (DE) Director-General
Generaldirektor (DE) General Manager
Generaldirektør (DK NO) Director-General
Generaldirektør (DK) General Manager
Generaldirektör (SE) Director-General
Gérant (FR) Director; Managing/Factory/General
   Manager
Gerente (ES) Manager
Gerente bancário (PT) Bank Manager
Geschäftsbereichsleiter (DE) Divisional Head/
   Manager
Geschäftsführender Direktor (DE) Managing
   Director
Geschäftstellenleiter (DE) Office Manager
Gestor de assuntos de organização (PT) Head of
   Organizational Development

Gestor financeiro (PT) Financial Manager
Gestor de produto (PT) Product Manager
Gevolmachtigde (NL) Executive Assistant
Giornalista (IT) Journalist
Giurista bancario (IT) Legal Adviser (Bank)
G.M. (GB) General Manager
Group Managing Director (GB) President (CEO)

H

Handelsvertegenwoordiger (NL) Commercial/Sales
   Representative
Handelsvertreter (DE) Commercial/Sales
   Representative
Head of Administration (GB) Director of
   Administration
Head of Chancellery (GB) Deputy Chief of Mission
Head of Police (GB) Chief of Police
Head of Security (GB) Chief of Security Section/
   Department/Division
Head of Staff Section/Department/Division (GB)
   Chief of Staff
Head of Organisational Planning (GB) Head of
   Organizational Development
Headmaster/Headmistress (GB) Principal
Hoofd (NL) Head/Chief/Senior/Manager
Hoofd A.G.V. (NL) (NL) Computer/Data
   Processing Manager
Hoofd administratie (NL) Head of Administration
Hoofd administratieafdeling (NL) Manager of
   Administration
Hoofd automatische gegevensverwerking (NL)
   Computer/Data Processing Manager
Hoofd contractafdeling (NL) Contracts Manager
Hoofd dienst opleiding (NL) Chief Training Officer
Hoofd distributie (NL) Distribution Manager
Hoofd divisie (NL) Divisional Manager
Hoofd expeditieafdeling (NL) Shipping
   (Department) Manager
Hoofd exportafdeling (NL) Export Manager
Hoofd financiële afdeling (NL) Chief Financial
   Officer; Head of Financial Section/Financial
   Manager
Hoofd informaticadienst (NL) Computer/Data
   Processing Manager
Hoofd klantendienst (NL) Head of Customer
   Service; Service Manager
Hoofd logistiek (NL) Logistics Manager
Hoofd onderzoeksafdeling (NL) Research Manager
Hoofd ontwikkelingsafdeiling (NL) Drafting Office
   Manager; Development Manager
Hoofd organisatieafdeling (NL) Head of
   Organizational Development
Hoofd planningsafdeling (NL) Director of Planning

Hoofd publiciteit (NL) Advertising Manager/
Director
Hoofd reclame (NL) Advertising Manager/
Director
Hoofd sectie (NL) Head of (the...) Section/
Department/Division
Hoofd systeemafdeling (NL) Systems Manager
Hoofd transport afdeling (NL) Transportation
Section/Department/Division Manager
Hoofd veiligheidsdienst (NL) Safety/Security
Manager
Hoofd verkoop (NL) Marketing Director
Hoofdaccountant (NL) Chief/Senior/Head
Accountant
Hoofdboekhouder (NL) Chief/Senior/Head
Accountant
Hoofdingenieur (NL) Chief Engineer
Hoofdredacteur (NL) Editor-in-Chief
Hovedbogholder (DK) Chief Accountant

I

Indkøber (DK) Buyer/Purchaser
Indkøbschef (DK) Purchasing Manager; Chief/
Head Buyer/Purchaser
Informasjonsdirektør (NO) Director of Public
Relations
Informationsdirektör (SE) Director of Public
Relations
Informationsdirektør (DK) Director of Public
Relations
Ingegnere (IT) ...Engineer
Ingegnere capo (IT) Chief Engineer
Ingegnere di manutenzione (IT) Maintenance
Engineer
Ingegnere sistemista (IT) Systems Engineer
Ingegnere tecnicocommerciale (IT) Sales Engineer
Ingegnere di sviluppo (IT) Development Engineer
Ingegnere Ufficio brevetti (IT) Patent Engineer
Ingenier onderhoudsafdeling (NL) Maintenance
Engineer
Ingeniero Comercial (ES) Sales Engineer
Ingeniero de Mantenimiento (ES) Maintenance
Engineer
Ingeniero (ES) ...Engineer
Ingeniero de Desarrollo (ES) Development
Engineer
Ingeniero de Patentes (ES) Patent Engineer
Ingeniero Jefe (ES) Chief Engineer
Ingeniero Proyectista (ES) Design Engineer
Ingénieur (de) développement (FR) Development
Engineer
Ingénieur (FR) ...Engineer
Ingenieur (NL DE) ...Engineer
Ingénieur commercial (FR) Sales Engineer

Ingénieur de brevets (FR) Patent Engineer
Ingénieur de maintenance (FR) Maintenance
Engineer
Ingénieur en chef (FR) Chief Engineer
Ingénieur-projeteur (FR) Design Engineer
Ingeniør (DK NO) ...Engineer
Ingenjör (SE) ...Engineer
Inkoopchef (NL) Chief/Head Buyer/Purchaser;
Purchasing Manager
Inköpare (SE) Purchaser
Inkoper (NL) Purchaser/Buyer
Inköpschef (SE) Purchasing Manager
Inköpare (SE) Buyer
Inköpschef (SE) Chief/Head Buyer/Purchaser
Innkjøper (NO) Buyer/Purchaser
Innkjøpssjef (NO) Purchasing Manager
Innenrevisor (DE) Internal Auditor
Innkjøpssjef (NO) Chief/Head Buyer/Purchaser
Inspecteur (NL FR) Inspector; Surveyor
Inspecteur-general bij de douane (NL) Director of
Customs
Inspector (PT ES) Inspector; Surveyor
Inspektor (DE) Inspector; Surveyor
Inspektør (DK NO) Inspector; Surveyor; Instructor
Inspektör (SE) Inspector; Surveyor; Instructor
Instructeur (NL FR) Instructor
Instructor (ES) Instructor
Instruktør (DK) Instructor
Instrutor (PT) Instructor
Intermediatore (IT) Broker
Intern revisor (DK) Internal Auditor
Interne audit (NL) Internal Auditor
Internrevisor (NO SE) Internal Auditor
Ispettore (IT) Inspector; Surveyor
Istruttore (IT) Instructor
IT-sjef (NO) Systems Manager

J

Jefe (ES) Head/Chief/Senior/Manager
Jefe Administrativo (ES) Manager of
Administration
Jefe de Aduana (ES) Customs Director
Jefe de Almacén (ES) Warehouse Supervisor
Jefe de Compras (ES) Chief/Head Buyer/
Purchaser; Purchasing Manager
Jefe de Contabilidad (ES) Chief/Senior/Head
Accountant
Jefe de Contratos (ES) Contracts Manager
Jefe de División (ES) Divisional Head/Manager
Jefe de Embarques (ES) Shipping (Department)
Manager
Jefe de Expedición (ES) Shipping (Department)
Manager

Jefe de Exportación (ES) Export Manager
Jefe de Gestión Inmobiliaria (ES) Real Estate
  Manager
Jefe de Investigación (ES) Research Manager
Jefe de la Planificación Administrativa (ES) Head
  of Organizational Development
Jefe de Laboratorio (ES) Laboratory Manager
Jefe de Logística (ES) Logistics Manager
Jefe de Mantenimiento (ES) Service Manager
Jefe de Oficina (ES) Office Manager
Jefe de Personal (ES) Staff Manager
Jefe de Producto (ES) Product Manager
Jefe de Proyecto(s) (ES) Project Officer
Jefe de Sistemas (ES) Systems Manager
Jefe de Transportes (ES) Transportation Section/
  Department/Division Manager
Jefe de Ventas (ES) Sales Manager; Distribution
  Manager
Jefe de(l) Departamento (ES) Head of (the ...)
Jefe del Departamento de Desarrollo (ES)
  Development Manager
Jefe del Gabinete de Estudios (ES) Drafting Office
  Manager
Jefe del Gabinete de Proyectos (ES) Drafting Office
  Manager
Jefe del Servicio Antiincendio (ES) Fire Marshal
Jefe del Servicio Control de Calidad (ES) Head of
  Quality Control
Jefe del Servicio de Personal (ES) Head of Staff
Jefe del Servicio de Seguridad (ES) Head of Safety/
  Security
Jefe del Servicio Control de Calidad (ES) Quality
  Control Manager
Jefe del Servicio de Mantenimiento (ES) Service
  Manager
Jefe del Servicio de Ventas (ES) Sales Manager
Jefe del Servicio Informático (ES) Computer/Data
  Processing Manager
Jefe del Servicio Local de Policía (ES) Chief of
  Police
Jefe del Servicio Post-ventas (ES) Head of
  Customer Service
Jefe Departamental (ES) Departmental Manager
Jefe Publicidad (ES) Advertising Manager/Director
Jornalista (PT) Journalist
Journalist (DK NL DE NO SE) Journalist
Journaliste (FR) Journalist
Juridisk rådgiver (NO) Legal Adviser (Company)
Jurist (SE) Lawyer/Attorney
Juriste bancaire (FR) Legal Adviser (Bank)

K
Kamrer (SE) Chief/Senior/Head Accountant

Kanselarijhoofd (NL) Deputy Chief of Mission
Kanslichef (SE) Director of Administration; Deputy
  Chief of Mission
Kantoorchef (NL) Office Manager
Kanzleivorsteher (DE) Deputy Chief of Mission
Kommunstyrelsens ordförande (SE) Mayor
Koncernchef (DK SE) President (CEO); Group
  Managing Director
Konsernsjef (NO) President (CEO); Group
  Managing Director
Konstruksjonssjef (NO) Drafting Office Manager
Konstrukteur (DE) Design Engineer
Konstruktionschef (DK SE) Drafting Office
  Manager
Konstruktionsleiter (DE) Drafting Office Manager
Konstruktør (DK NO) Design Engineer
Konstruktör (SE) Design Engineer
Konsul (DK DE NO SE) Consul
Konsulent (DK NO) Consultant
Konsult (SE) Consultant
Kontorchef (DK) Office Manager
Kontorschef (SE) Office Manager
Kontorsjef (NO) Office Manager
Kontraktchef (DK) Contracts Manager
Kontraktschef (SE) Head of Contracts
Kontraktschef (SE) Contracts Manager
Kontraktssjef (NO) Contracts Manager
Konzernchef (DE) President (CEO); Group
  Managing Director
Krankenhausdirektor (DE) Director of Medical
  (Hospital) Services
Kvalitetschef (DK SE) Quality Control Manager
Kvalitetssjef (NO) Quality Control Manager

L
Laboratoriechef (DK SE) Laboratory Manager
Laboratorieleder (DK) Laboratory Manager
Laboratoriesjef (NO) Laboratory Manager
Laboratoriumchef (NL) Laboratory Manager
Laborleiter (DE) Laboratory Manager
Læge (DK) Physician
Lagerchef (DK NO SE) Warehouse Supervisor
Lagerverwalter (DE) Warehouse Supervisor
Läkare (SE) Managing Director
Lector (NL) Lecturer
Lege (NO) Managing Director
Lagersjef (NO) Warehouse Supervisor
Lagerverwalter (DE) Warehouse Supervisor
Leder (DK) Head/Chief/Senior
Lege (NO) Managing Director
Leitender Direktor (DE) General Manager
Leitender Ingenieur (DE) Chief Engineer
Leiter (DE) Head/Chief/Senior/Manager

Leiter der Abteilung Öffentlichkeitsarbeit (DE)
Public Relations Manager
Leiter der Abteilung für Vertragsfragen (DE)
Contracts Manager
Leiter der Buchhaltung (DE) Chief/Senior/Head
Accountant
Leiter der EDV-Abteilung (DE) Computer/Data
Processing/Systems Manager
Leiter der Einkaufsabteilung (DE) Chief/Head
Buyer/Purchaser
Leiter der Entwicklungsabteilung (DE)
Development Manager
Leiter der Exportabteilung (DE) Director/Manager
of Export Section/Department/Division
Leiter der Finanz- und Rechnungswesens (DE)
Financial Manager
Leiter der Finanzabteilung (DE) Chief Financial
Officer; Director of Finance; Financial Manager
Leiter der Forschungsabteilung (DE) Director of
Research
Leiter der Konstruktionsabteilung (DE) Drafting
Office Manager
Leiter der Kundendienstabteilung (DE) Head of
Customer Service
Leiter der Kundendienstabteilung (DE) Service
Manager
Leiter der Marketingabteilung (DE) Marketing
Director
Leiter der PR-Abteilung (DE) Public Relations
Officer
Leiter der Schulungsabteilung (DE) Chief Training
Officer
Leiter der Versandabteilung (DE) Shipping
(Department) Manager
Leiter der Werbeabteilung (DE) Advertising
Manager/Director
Leiter des Aus- und Forbildungswesens (DE) Chief
Training Officer
Leiter des Qualitätswesens (DE) Quality Control
Manager
Leiter des Rechenzentrums (DE) Head of
Computer/Data Processing/Systems Section/
Department/Division
Leiter/Direktor der Betriebsorganisation (DE)
Head of Organizational Development
Leiter/Direktor der Finanzabteilung (DE) Financial
Manager/Head of Financial Section
Leiter/Direktor der Frachtabteilung (DE)
Transportation Section/Department/Division
Manager
Leiter/Direktor der Grundstücksverwaltung (DE)
Real Estate Manager
Leiter/Direktor der Logistikabteilung (DE)
Logistics Manager

Leiter/Direktor der Organisationsabteilung (DE)
Head of Organizational Development; Sales
Manager
Leiter/Direktor der Personalabteilung (DE) Staff
Manager; Chief of Staff
Leiter/Direktor der Planungsabteilung (DE)
Director of Planning
Leiter/Direktor der Transportabteilung (DE)
Transportation Section/Department/Division
Manager
Leiter/Direktor der Versandabteilung (DE)
Transportation Section/Department/Division
Manager
Leiter/Direktor des Zollamts (DE) Customs
Director
Leiter/Direktor der Zollstelle (DE) Customs
Director
Leiter der Werbeabteilung (DE) Advertising
Director/Manager
Lektor (DE) Lecturer
Logistikchef (DK SE) Logistics Manager
Logistikksjef (NO) Logistics Manager

M
M.D. (GB) Managing Director
Mægler (DK) Broker
Magazijnbeheerder (NL) Warehouse Supervisor
Maire (FR) Mayor
Maître de conférences (FR) Lecturer
Makelaar (NL) Broker
Mäklare (SE) Broker
Makler (DE) Broker
Managing Director (GB) President (CEO)
Markedassistent (NO) Assistant/Deputy
Marketing Manager
Markedsdirektør (NO) Director of Marketing
Marketing (en sales) manager (NL) Marketing (and
Sales) Manager
Marketingassistent (DK) Assistant Marketing
Manager
Marketing directeur (NL) Marketing Director
Marketingassistent (DK) Assistant/Deputy
Marketing Manager
Marketingdirektør (DK) Director of Marketing
Marketingleiter (DE) Director of Marketing
Marknadsassistent (SE) Assistant/Deputy
Marketing Manager
Marknadsdirektör (SE) Marketing Director
Médecin (FR) Physician
Medhjælpende ... (DK) Assistant ... /Deputy...
Medico (IT) Physician
Médico (PT ES) Physician
Médico dentista (PT) Dental Surgeon/Dentist

Megler (NO) Broker
Meister (DE) Foreman
Ministerio Fiscal (ES) Prosecutor
Ministerio Público (ES) Prosecutor

N

Näringslivssekreterare (SE) Project Officer
Næringsutviklinskonsulent (NO) Project Officer
Notaire (FR) Notary Public
Notar (DE) Notary Public
Notario (IT ES) Notary Public
Notário Público (PT) Notary Public
Notaris (NL) Notary Public
Notarius publicus (DK NO SE) Notary Public
Novedbogholder (DK) Chief/Senior/Head
   Accountant

O

Oberbuchhalter (DE) Chief/Senior/Head
   Accountant
Oberingenieur (DE) Chief Engineer
Oberstudiendirektor (DE) Principal
Octrooitechnicus (NL) Patent Engineer
Ontwerpingenieur (NL) Design Engineer
Ontwikkelingsingenieur (NL) Development
   Engineer
Opplæringssjef (NO) Chief Training Officer
Ordförande (SE) Chairman/person
Ordfører (NO) Chairman/person; Mayor
Ordstyrer (NO) Chairman/person
Organisasjonssjef (NO) Head of Organizational
   Development
Organisationschef (DK SE) Head of Organizational
   Development
Overingeniør (DK NO) Chief Engineer
Overseer (GB) Supervisor
Økonomichef (DK) Chief Financial Officer /
   Manager
Økonomidirektør (DK NO) Chief Financial Officer;
   Director of Finance
Økonomisjef (NO) Chief Financial Officer /
   Manager
Överingenjör (SE) Chief Engineer

P

Patentingenieur (DE) Patent Engineer
Patentingeniør (DK NO) Patent Engineer
Patentingenjör (SE) Patent Engineer
Periodista (ES) Journalist
Perito contabile (IT) Chief/Senior/Head
   Accountant
Personalchef (DE SE) Head of Staff Section/
   Department/Division

Personalchef (DE) Personnel/Staff Director
Personalchef (DK DE SE) Staff Manager
Personaldirektør (DK NO) Staff Director
Personaldirektør (NO) Personnel Director
Personaldirektör (SE) Personnel/Staff Director
Personaledirektør (DK) Personnel Director
Personalleiter (DE) Staff Manager
Personalleiter/direktor (DE) Head of Staff
   Section/Department/Division
Personalsjef (NO) Head of Staff Section/
   Department/Division
Personalsjef (NO) Staff Manager
Personeeschef (NL) Staff Manager
Pharmacien (FR) Pharmacist
Plaatsvervangend ... (NL) Assistant ...
Planeringsdirektör (SE) Director of Planning
   Section/Department/Division
Planlægnings-direktør (DK) Director of Planning
   Section/Department/Division
Planleggingsdirektør (NO) Director of Planning
   Section/Department/Division
Planeringsdirektör (SE) Planning Director
Planlægningsdirektør (DK) Planning Director
Planleggingsdirektør (NO) Planning Director
Platschef (SE) Branch Manager
Ploegbaas (NL) Foreman; Master Mechanic;
   Supervisor
Polier (Bauindustrie) (DE) Foreman
Polischef (SE) Chief of Police
Politichef (DK) Chief of Police
Politimester (NO) Chief of Police
Polizeipräsident (DE) Chief of Police
Praktikant (DK DE NO SE) Trainee
Präsident (DE) Chairman/person
PR-Direktor (DE) Director of Public Relations
Preside (IT) Vice-Chancellor
Preside (IT) Principal
Président (FR) Chairman/person
President (NL) Chairman/person
Président du conseil d'administration (FR)
   Chairman of the Board (of Directors)
Président du groupe (FR) President (CEO); Group
   Managing Director
Président-directeur général (FR) President (CEO)
   Group Managing Director; Chairman of the
   Board (of Directors)
Président-directeur général (FR) President (CEO)
   Group Managing Director/General Manager/
   Managing Director
Presidente (IT PT ES) Chaiman/person
Presidente de grupo empresarial (PT) President
   (CEO); Group Managing Director

Presidente del Consejo de Administración (ES)
Chairman of the Board (of Directors)
Presidente del consiglio di amministrazione (IT)
Chairman of the Board (of Directors)
Presidente del Grupo (IT ES) President (CEO);
Group Managing Director
Presidente do Conselho de Administração (PT)
Chairman of the Board (of Directors)
Pressechef (DE) Director of Public Relations
(P.R./Information)
Pressesprecher (DE) Director of Public Relations
(P.R./Information)
Procurador (PT) Executive Assistant
Procuratiehouder (NL) Executive Assistant
Procuratore (IT) Executive Assistant
Procuratore della Repubblica (IT) Prosecutor
Procureur (NL FR) Prosecutor
Product manager (NL) Product Manager
Produksjonssjef (NO) Production Director
Produktchef (DK SE) Product Manager
Produktierdirecteur (NL) Production Director
Produktionsdirektør (DK) Production Director
Produktionsdirektör (SE) Production Director
Produktionsleder (DK) Production Director
Produktmanager (DE) Product Manager
Produktsjef (NO) Product Manager
Profesor (ES) Professor
Professeur (FR) Professor
Professor (DK NL DE NO PT SE) Professor
Professor) Agregado (ES) Reader
Professore (IT) Professor
Production Manager (NL) Production Director/
Manager
Progettista (IT) Design Engineer
Programador (ES PT) Programmer
Programmatore (IT) Programmer
Programmerare (SE) Programmer
Programmerer (NO) Programmer
Programmeur (FR NL) Programmer
Programmierer (DE) Programmer
Programmør (DK) Programmer
Projektledare (SE) Project Leader/Manager
Projektleder (DK) Project Leader/Manager
Projectleider (NL) Project Leader/Manager
Projektleiter (DE) Project Leader/Manager
Prokurist (DK DE NO SE) Executive Assistant
Prosjektleder (NO) Project Leader/Manager
Prüfer (DE) Inspector

Q

Questore (IT) Chief of Police

R
Raadsman (NL) Consultant
Rådgiver (NO) Consultant
Rappresentante (IT) Commercial/Sales
Representative
Reader (GB) Lecturer
Rechtsanwalt (DE) Lawyer/Attorney
Rechtskundig adviseur bij een bedrijf (NL) Legal
Adviser (Company)
Rechtskundig bankadviseur (NL) Legal Adviser
(Bank)
Recteur (FR) Vice-Chancellor
Rector (ES) Vice-Chancellor
Rector (NL) Principal; Vice-Chancellor
Rector (Escuela) (ES) Principal
Rédacteur en chef (FR) Editor-in-Chief
Redactor de textos de publicidade (PT) Copywriter
Redactor Jefe (ES) Editor-in-Chief
Redactor Planificador (ES) Copywriter
Redactor-chefe (PT) Editor-in-Chief
Redattore capo (IT) Editor-in-Chief
Redattore di testi pubblicitari (IT) Copywriter
Redovisningschef (SE) Chief/Senior/Head
Accountant
Referatsleiter (DE) Departmental Manager
Referent für Unternehmensberatung (DE) Project
Officer
Regionale chef/directeur (NL) Regional Director/
Manager
Regionchef (SE) Regional Director/Manager
Regionschef (DK) Regional Director/Manager
Regionsjef (NO) Regional Director/Manager
Regnskapssjef (NO) Chief/Senior/Head
Accountant
Reitor (PT) Vice-Chancellor
Reklamchef (SE) Advertising Manager/Director
Reklamechef (DK) Advertising Manager/Director
Reklamesjef (NO) Advertising Manager/Director
Rektor (DK DE NO SE) Principal; Vice-Chancellor
Repræsentant (DK) Commercial/Sales
Representative
Représentant (FR) Sales Representative
Representant (NO) Sales Representative
Représentant de commerce (FR) Sales
Representative
Representante (PT) Sales Representative
Representante do Ministério Público (PT)
Prosecutor
Representant (NO SE) Commercial Representative
Représentant de commerce (FR) Commercial
Representative
Representante (PT) Commercial Representative

Representante (ES) Agent
Responsabile (IT) Manager
Responsabile delle commesse (IT) Contracts
  Manager
Responsabile dello stabilimento (IT) Supervisor
Responsabile des contrats (FR) Head of Contracts
Responsabile finanziario (IT) Financial Manager
Responsabile formazione (IT) Chief Training
  Officer
Responsabile prodotti (IT) Product Manager
Responsabile magazzini (IT) Warehouse
  Supervisor
Responsabile servizio EDP (IT) Computer/Data
  Processing Manager
Responsabile servizio marketing e vendite (IT)
  Marketing (and Sales)
Responsabile Sicurezza (IT) Head of Safety/
  Security Section/Department/Division
Responsabile sviluppo (IT) Development Manager
Responsabile transporti (IT) Transportation
  Section/Department/Division Manager
Responsabile vendite (IT) Sales Manager
Responsabile/Capo del progetto (IT) Project
  Leader/Manager
Responsable administratif (FR) Manager of
  Administration
Responsable de projet (FR) Project Leader/
  Manager
Responsable de la formation (FR) Head of Training
Responsable de la publicité (FR) Advertising
  Manager/Director
Responsable système(s) (FR) Systems Manager
Rettore (IT) Principal; Vice-Chancellor
Revisor (DK NL DE NO SE) Auditor
Revisor (NO SE) Accountant
Revisor de contas (PT) Auditor
Revisor interno (PT) Internal Auditor
Revisore (IT) Auditor
Revisore interno (IT) Internal Auditor

S
Säkerhetschef (SE) Safety/Security Manager
Sælger (DK) Sales Representative; Salesman
Salgschef (DK) Sales/Marketing/Distribution
  Manager
Salgsingeniør (DK NO) Sales Engineer
Salgsleder (DK NO) Sales Manager
Salgssjef (NO) Sales Manager
Säljare (SE) Sales Representative; Salesman
Säljledare (SE) Sales Manager
Salgsdirectør (DK NO) Distribution Director;
  Director of Sales
Salgssjef (NO) Distribution/Marketing (and Sales)
  Manager

Schoolhoofd (NL) Principal
Schriftführer (DE) Secretary
Schulungsleiter (DE) Chief Training Officer
Secrétaire (FR) Secretary
Secrétaire á la promotion des enterprises (FR)
  Project Officer
Secrétaire d'administration (FR) *(Public
  Administration)* Assistant Director
Secrétaire de direction (FR) Personal Assistant;
  Senior Executive Secretary
Secretario (ES) Secretary
Secretário (PT) Secretary
Secretario de Dirección (ES) Personal Assistant ;
  Senior Executive Secretary
Secretario de Estado (ES) Permanent Secretary
Secretário de Estado (PT) Permanent Secretary
Secretário do Director-Geral (PT) Personal
  Assistant;   Senior Executive Secretary
Secretaris (NL) Secretary
Sectiehoofd (NL) Secretary
Segretario (IT) Secretary
Segretario Amministratore delegato (IT) Senior
  Executive Secretary
Segretario dell'Industria (IT) Project Officer
Segretario dello Stato (IT) Permanent Secretary
Sekretær (DK NO) Secretary
Sekretär (DE) Secretary
Sekretär der Geschäftsleitung (DE) Personal
  Assistant; Senior Executive Secretary
Sekrétaire d'Etat (FR) Permanent Secretary
Sekretariatschef (DK) Director of Administration;
  Deputy Chief of Mission
Sekreterare (SE) Secretary
Selger (NO) Sales Representative/Salesman
Selger (NO) Commercial Representative
Senior (Managing/Signing/Confidential) Clerk (G
  Executive Assistant
Service Engineer (GB) Maintenance Engineer
Serviceingeniør (DK NO) Maintenance Engineer
Serviceingenjör (SE) Maintenance Engineer
Servicesjef (NO) Service Manager; Head of
  Customer Service
Shippingchef (DK) Shipping (Department)
  Manager
Sikkerhedschef (DK) Safety/Security Manager;
  Chief of Security
Sikkerhetssjef (NO) Safety/Security Manager;
  Chief of Security
Sindaco (IT) Mayor
Sjef (NO) Head/Chief/Senior/Manager
Sjefredaktør (NO) Editor-in-Chief
Sjefssekretær (NO) Personal Assistant to the
  General Manager; Personal Assistant; Senior
  Executive Secretary

jukhusdirektör (SE) Director of Medical (Hospital) Services
keppningschef (SE) Shipping (Department) Manager
.M. (GB) Sales Manager
olicitor (GB) Lawyer/Attorney
ous-directeur (FR) *(Public Administration)* Deputy Director
ous-directeur de ... (FR) *(Public Administration)* Head of (the ...) Section/Department/Division
pediteur (DE) Freight Forwarder; Shipping Agent
peditør (DK NO) Freight Forwarder; Shipping Agent
peditör (SE) Freight Forwarder; Shipping Agent
pedizioniere (IT) Freight Forwarder; Shipping Agent
taatsanwalt (DE) Prosecutor
taatssecretaris (NL) Permanent Secretary
taatssekretär (DE) Permanent Secretary
tatsadvokat (NO) Prosecutor
tatssekretær (DK) Permanent Secretary
tatssekreterare (SE) Permanent Secretary
tellvertrender Direktor (DE) Assistant/Deputy Director
tellvertretender Generaldirektor (DE) Vice President; Deputy General Manager; Managing Director
tellvertretender ... (DE) Assistant ... ; Deputy ...
tores Manager (GB) Warehouse Supervisor
tyreformann (NO) Chairman of the Board (of Directors)
tyrelseordförande (SE) Chairman of the Board (of Directors)
ubdirector (ES) Vice President; Deputy General Manager; Managing Director
upervisor de projecto (PT) Project Leader/Manager
ygehusdirektør (DK) Director of Medical (Hospital) Services
ykehusdirektør (NO) Hospital Director/Manager
ysteemanalist (NL) Systems Analyst/Engineer
ystemanalytiker (DE) Systems Analyst
ystemansvarlig (DK) Systems Analyst/Engineer
ystemansvarlig (NO) Systems Engineer
ystemerare (SE) Systems Analyst/Engineer
ystemerer (NO) Systems Engineer
ystemprogrammierer (DE) Systems Engineer
ystemschef (DK) Systems Manager
ystemchef (SE) Systems Manager
ystemsjef (NO) Systems Manager
, suppléant (FR) Assistant ...

T
Tandarts (NL) Dental Surgeon; Dentist
Tandlæge (DK) Dental Surgeon; Dentist
Tandläkare (SE) Dental Surgeon; Dentist
Tannlege (NO) Dental Surgeon; Dentist
Technicien d'entretien (FR) Maintenance Engineer
Technisch directeur (NL) Technical Director
Technisch verkoper (NL) Sales Engineer
Technischer Leiter/Direktor (DE) Technical Director
Tecnico (IT) ... Engineer
Tecnico addetto allo sviluppo (IT) Development Engineer
Tecnico di manutenzione (IT) Maintenance Engineer
Tegnestueleder (DK) Drafting Office Manager
Teknisk chef (SE) Plant Manager; Technical Director
Teknisk direktør (DK NO) Technical Director
Teknisk direktør (NO) Plant Manager
Teknisk direktör (SE) Plant Manager; Technical Director
Teknisk sjef (NO) Plant Manager; Technical Director
Tekstforfatter (NO) Copywriter
Tierarzt (DE) Veterinarian
Toldchef (DK) Director of Customs
Tollsjef (NO) Director of Customs
Transportchef (DK SE) Transportation Section/Department/Division Manager
Transportsjef (NO) Shipping (Department) Manager
Transportsjef (NO) Transportation/Shipping Section/Department/Division Manager
Tullchef (SE) Director of Customs

U
Uddannelsesleder (DK) Chief Training Officer
Udviklingschef (DK) Development Manager
Udviklingsingeniør (DK) Development Engineer
Underdirektør (NO) Deputy Director
Universitetslektor (NO SE) Lecturer
Unternehmensberater (DE) Legal Adviser (Company)
Utbildningschef (SE) Chief Training Officer
Utvecklingschef (SE) Development Manager
Utvecklingsingenjör (SE) Development Engineer
Utviklingsingeniør (NO) Development Engineer
Utviklingssjef (NO) Development Manager

V
Værkfører (DK) Master Mechanic; Supervisor
Vendedor (ES/PT) Salesman

Vendeur (FR) Sales Representative; Salesman
Venditore (IT) Salesman
Verkäufer (DE) Sales Representative; Salesman
Verkaufsingenieur (DE) Sales Engineer
Verkaufsleiter (DE) Sales Manager /Director;
Distribution Manager
VD-sekreterare (SE) Personal Assistant to the
General Manager
Verkaufsleiter (DE) Director of Sales (Marketing)
Section/Department/Division
Verkaufsleiter/direktor (DE) Distribution Manager
Verkmästare (SE) Master Mechanic; Supervisor
Verkoopchef (NL) Distribution Manager; Sales
Manager
Verkoopdirecteur (NL) Director of Sales
(Marketing) Section/Department/Division
Verkoper (NL) Salesman
Verkschef (SE) Factory/Plant Manager
Verksmester (NO) Master Mechanic; Supervisor
Verkssjef (NO) Factory/Plant Manager
Verkställande direktör (SE) General Manager
Vertegenwoordiger (NL) Agent
Vertreter (DE) Agent
Vertriebsingenieur (DE) Sales Engineer
Vertriebsleiter (DE) Sales Manager; Distribution
Director
Verwaltungsdirektor (DE) Director of
Administration
Verwaltungsratsvorsitzender (DE) Chairman of the
Board (of Directors)
Veterinær (NO) Veterinarian
Vétérinaire (FR) Veterinarian
Veterinär (SE) Veterinarian
Veterinario (IT ES) Veterinarian
Veterinário (PT) Veterinarian
Veterinary Officer/Surgeon (GB) Veterinarian
Vice-Director (PT) Assistant/Deputy Director
Vice-generaldirektør (DK) Vice President; Deputy
General Manager; Managing Director
Vice verkställande direktör (SE) Vice President;
Deputy General/Managing Manager
Vice-gerente (PT) Vice President; Deputy Managing
Director
Vice ... (IT) Deputy ...
Viceamministratore delegato (IT) Deputy
Managing Director
Vicedirektør (DK) Assistant/Deputy Director
Vicedirettore (IT) Assistant/Deputy Director
Vicedirettore generale (IT) Deputy General
Manager
Vicegerente (ES) Vice President; Deputy General
Manager/Managing Director
Vice ... (IT) Assistant ...

Vise ... (NO) Deputy ...;Assistant ...
Viseadministrerende direktør (NO) Vice President;
Deputy General Manager; Managing Director
Voorman (NL) Foreman/Master Mechanic/
Supervisor
Voorzitter (NL) Chairman/person
Voorzitter van de raad van beheer (NL) Chairman
of the Board (of Directors)
Voorzitter (van een concern) (NL) President (CEO);
Group Managing Director
Vorarbeiter (DE) Foreman; Supervisor
Vorarbeiter Mechanikermeister (DE) Master
Mechanic
Vorsitzender (DE) Chairman/person
Vorstandsvorsitzender (DE) Chairman of the Board
(of Directors)

W

Wartungsingenieur (DE) Maintenance Engineer
Wartungstechniker (DE) Maintenance Engineer
Werbetexter (DE) Copywriter
Weksleiter (DE) Factory Manager
Werkmeister (DE) Foreman; Master Mechanic;
Supervisor
Werkschutzleiter (DE) Head of Safety/Security
Section/Department/Division
Werkschutzleiter (DE) Safety/Security Manager;
Chief of Security
Werkschutzleiter (DE) Security Manager
Werksdirektor (DE) Factory/Plant Manager
Wirtschaftsprüfer (DE) Auditor/Internal Auditor
Works Manager (GB) Factory Manager

Z

Zahnarzt (DE) Dental Surgeon; Dentist
Ziekenhuisdirecteur (NL) Director of
Medical (Hospital) Services
Zweigstellenleiter (DE) Branch Manager

General Index

*IBC—Indicates information is found on the Inside Back Cover.

134

*IBC—Indicates information is found on the Inside Back Cover.

95893

---

*IBC—Indicates reference is found on the Inside Back Cover.